The Republic

The Republic

Consultant editor
MARY JONES
ArkHive Productions

THE THOMAS DAVIS LECTURE SERIES
Series Producer: Peter Mooney

Published in association with

MERCIER PRESS
Douglas Village, Cork
www.mercierpress.ie

Trade enquiries to CMD DISTRIBUTION,
55a Spruce Avenue, Stillorgan Industrial Park, Blackrock, Dublin

ISBN 1 85635 490 3

10 9 8 7 6 5 4 3 2 1

Front cover photograph of Áras an Uachtaráin
reproduced by kind permission of the
Department of Environment, Heritage and Local Government

Mercier Press receives financial assistance from
the Arts Council/An Chomhairle Ealaíon

Printed and Bound by J. H. Haynes & Co. Ltd. Sparkford

Contents

Foreword   7
Eunan O'Halpin

Introduction: Ancient Republics   9
   and other Political Dreams
Marianne McDonald

1 – Reclaiming the Republican Tradition   25
Iseult Honohan

2 – Theobald Wolfe Tone and   42
   Irish Republicanism and Separatism
Thomas Bartlett

3 – The Easter Proclamation of 1916 and   58
   the Democratic Programme
Martin Mansergh

4 – James Connolly and   75
   the Worker's Republic
Brian Hanley

5 – The Unreal Republic   88
Fintan O'Toole

6 – Law in a Republic   102
Ivana Bacik

7 – Republic: a Hope Mislaid?   119
Mary Kotsonouris

8 – From Republican Theory   130
    to Public Policy
Philip Pettit

The Contributors   148

Notes   150

Foreword

Eunan O'Halpin

In his concluding contribution to this volume, the distinguished political philosopher Philip Pettit writes that 'the Republic is too important to be left to the historians'. He need not have worried, although even history can have its uses.

The editor has ensured that the complex, enduring, evolving and contested concepts of 'The Republic' are addressed from a range of disciplines and perspectives. All the contributors, two themselves involved in national politics, are Irish or have Irish connections, but their themes are far broader. While *The Republic* has specifically Irish resonances it is rooted in the evolution of political ideas and aspirations which have developed over millennia and which have become intertwined with related concepts – national self-determination, democracy, socialism, individual liberty, the rule of law, equality, socialism – not all of which always lie easily together. Ask any unionist.

Must 'The Republic' be embodied in an explicit constitutional form? The most sustained transformative efforts to construct independent, fair, prosperous, equal, democratic

and lawbound societies in the twentieth century were probably those of the Scandinavian states, yet Denmark, Sweden
and Norway are all monarchies.

By contrast, some recent adherents to republican forms –
the pariah statelet, Republica Srbska, built explicitly on a
foundation of ethnic hatred, the benighted Democratic Republic of the Congo, the theocratic Islamic Republic of Iran
– demonstrate that the term 'Republic' alone is no guide to
either the nature or the aspirations of polities. Yet the
divisions within the independence movement which led to
the Irish civil war largely evolved around the issue of whether
true freedom could be secured without 'The Republic' in
name as well as in form. That is why my mother's father fought
against the Treaty; yet my father's father, exiled from Northern Ireland in 1922, joined the police force of the new Free
State. Both considered themselves Irish republicans, and
they were both right.

EUNAN O'HALPIN
Professor of Contemporary Irish History
Trinity College

Introduction

Ancient Republics and other Political Dreams

Marianne McDonald

What is the good life? What political system best allows the pursuit of happiness? Does the system we call democracy play a significant role, or is it a hindrance? What is the role of ethics? These questions have never been more urgent than at the present moment when political ideologies and religions are battling for dominance with appalling consequences for human freedom. Like everything else in our western civilisation, attempts to answer these questions begin with the Greeks. After all, as the philosopher Alfred North Whitehead said, 'The safest general characterisation of the European philosophical tradition is that it consists of a series of footnotes to Plato.'[1] It's his vision in *The Republic* that offers some answers, but first we'll look at some of the predecessors of this fundamental work that has shaped so many of our modern political philosophies.[2]

The Republic

The Greeks came to democracy gradually in the late sixth century BC, following on some unpleasant experiences of tyranny. Nearly 200 years later, the philosophers Plato and Aristotle both had their doubts about democracy. Most moderns question the ancient Greek democracy because it extended only to male citizens and excluded women and resident aliens, besides sanctioning slavery. For more than a few centuries, the Romans had a viable republic, which tried to accommodate man's needs, but they lived under kings before that republic, and later they had emperors.

A republic itself is variously defined, but the one element we can abstract is that it is a representational democracy. Both Athenian democracy ('people in power') and the ancient Roman *res publica* ('public business') claimed that the 'people' were in charge, but the people chosen to run public business were a select group.

In this introductory essay let us look at the ideal political situations as described first of all by the eighth-century BC Greek poet Hesiod, and then by the fifth-century BC Greek tragedians, Aeschylus, Sophocles and Euripides. After this, we can investigate one of the comic playwright Aristophanes' views of Utopia: the *Ecclesiazusae* (about 392 BC), which described a society in which women are running the government and in which private property is divided and shared equally by all the citizens. All the evidence points to it coming earlier than Plato's *Republic* which is usually dated around 370 BC. All of these visions have modern relevance, and we ignore their ideas at our peril.

Hesiod had a fanciful vision of utopia, a word coined from the Greek by Thomas More in his work called *Utopia* in 1516. Greek etymology breaks the word down into two words: 'no place'. Utopia described where More's ideal society existed in his present world: nowhere, or at least not yet. Hesiod's utopia, as described in his *Works and Days*, could be equated with the golden age of long ago, when the gods allowed the men they created to live like themselves, without care, pain or suffering. Human beings did not grow old, but stayed youthful and strong, and enjoyed their feasts out of harm's way. They didn't have to work: the earth automatically provided them with food each year. They enjoyed freedom and lived in peace on their own lands with wealth sufficient to their needs, both in fruits of the earth and livestock. They were also beloved by the gods. When they died (painlessly in their sleep), they became holy spirits to watch over lawsuits and see when evil was committed.[3]

Hesiod's model for mankind's social evolution shows entropy in action, a gradual decline from the golden age to what suggests total annihilation. First, Zeus destroyed the men of the silver age, for impiety; then came the men of bronze, too warlike for their own good. This age was followed by the race of heroes. They also fought each other in battles, but the difference from the men of the bronze age is that they were called heroes and did not die nameless, but earned immortal fame in their pursuit of honour. This was the race that fostered Achilles, celebrated by Homer (about the second half of the eighth century BC) in his *Iliad*. Zeus rewarded these heroes and after death allowed them to live in the islands of the blessed where their needs were met by crops spontaneously growing, the same boon that men enjoyed during the golden age. Finally comes the iron age which for Hesiod is the present; he wishes he had lived either before or after. Men wear themselves out with work and suffering. We are told that Zeus will destroy this race when children are born with grey hair: this happened, in fact, to children born from parents who suffered from radiation following the bombing of Hiroshima and Nagasaki in 1945. Some ancient prophecies have shown themselves to be all too true.

Hesiod's description of what happens to the iron race sounds very much like modern times. The men of iron destroy each other's cities. Those who do the most wrong gain power and are the men who are most honoured. Criminals learn to lie and indict those who try to do what is right. Envy drives men to destroy their neighbours for the sheer pleasure of it. Shame and justice have flown away up to heaven. Now only suffering remains on earth. Hesiod follows this black vision with a plea for justice, urging that it provides the best way of life for man (128–221). In this he anticipates Plato's *Republic*.

Aeschylus, the first of the Greek tragedians, writing in the fifth century BC, presents a picture of progress in his *Prometheus Bound*. The ancient titan Prometheus is being punished for stealing fire from the gods and giving it to man. He explains to the chorus in the play that he found man in a state of ignorance rather like the iron generation just described, only without the viciousness. Promethean fire carried with it knowledge and passion for creativity. Prometheus lists what he taught men. Prometheus modestly concludes by saying: 'I taught man every skill he has'.[4] Since he gave men fire and banished their ignorance, the future is up to them. He has given them the tools for making a living. Now they had to learn how to live a life of quality, one that was both morally good and emotionally and intellectually satisfying.

In his *Eumenides*, the final play of the *Oresteia*, the only surviving trilogy from fifth century BC, Aeschylus tells us about the founding of the first law court with a jury at Athens. Orestes is tried in this play for killing his mother Clytemnestra, after she killed his father, Agamemnon. Apollo commanded him to do it, but Orestes has obviously committed matricide, and the goddesses of the earth who protect blood relatives, the Furies, object. The law of an eye for an eye and a tooth for a tooth is softened by what ought to be a more civilised approach, namely the establishment of a law court, and Orestes is acquitted by a vote. This is another symbolic affirmation of civilised progress.

One remembers Mahatma Gandhi, who advocated peaceful resistance, which in fact brought down the British empire in India, saying, 'An eye for eye only ends up making the whole world blind'.[5] When he was asked during his visit to England in 1930 what he thought of modern civilisation, he answered, 'That would be a good idea'.[6]

Sophocles in his *Antigone* (c. 440 BC), shows Creon taking over the kingship in Thebes after Polynices, the son of Oedipus, attacked the city to seize rule from his brother King Eteocles. When both brothers are killed, Creon orders a burial for Eteocles with all the honours, but forbids that Polynices be buried. Antigone, their sister, defies his decree, buries Polynices, and Creon condemns her to death.

Hegel pointed out that Antigone defends the rights of the family against the law of the government, since she thought that the law was unjust. Antigone claimed she was obeying the unwritten laws of the gods. One might call her the first civil disobedient. Sophocles may be telling us that personal rights, civil liberties, and also respect for the law must all be synthesised in a well-functioning and ethical city.

Sophocles' *Antigone* also describes man's progress: there are many wonders in the world, but nothing more amazing than man![7] Man now speaks of these discoveries as if they were his own. One can see the ode as an elaboration of Prometheus' gifts. Man has not only acquired technology and the skills for his physical needs, but also those for living well with other people: how to run a city, and how to run it well, namely with justice, not impelled by personal gain, but rather for mutual benefit. Another brick is added to the foundation of Plato's *Republic*.

Euripides, in his *Suppliants* (c. 422 BC), has Theseus, the King of Athens, protecting mothers who want to bury the bodies of their sons following the Theban war. In two speeches from this play, the virtues of democracy are opposed to the efficiency of tyranny. Theseus claims that his city Athens is not simply ruled by one man but that the people are free. They are in charge and take turns in office; and in this city the rich are not favoured over the poor. The Herald from Thebes, who claims that his city will go to war rather than turn the bodies over to their mothers, reproves Theseus by saying that he is pleased that his city *is* ruled by one man alone. He says, 'No one can flatter the people of Thebes and win them over for personal gain'.[8] He claims furthermore, the masses are ignorant: if they can't even compose a good speech, how can they run a city well? Men of high birth and merit cringe when they see a common person winning the support of the crowd simply by pandering to the desires of the masses (*Supp.*, pp. 409–425).

Theseus answers him by saying that a tyrant is the worst thing for a city. One man rules because he considers himself to be the law. In most cases this leads to injustice. If laws are written down, then both the poor and the rich have access to justice. They would both enjoy freedom of speech, *parrhesia*, a prized possession of democracy. A poor man can win over a rich man, if the right is on his side. This is the cornerstone of freedom. Anyone can bring a good proposal forward, and that man is praised for it (*Supp.*, pp. 429–441).

Aristophanes, the great ancient comic playwright, gives us a different vision of utopia when he shows women taking over the city in his play *Ecclesiazusae*, written at the beginning of the fourth century BC.[9] The women disguise themselves as men and vote themselves into power. It may very well be the first model for a gynaecocracy.

In his *Ecclesiazusae*, Aristophanes has Praxagora, an Athenian wife, leading her female friends in a coup, taking over the government and changing the society by abolishing private property and the institution of marriage. (*Ec.*, pp. 583–710.) All property goes into a communal pool from which the citizens are supported. Slaves do all the work, except that the female citizens are put in charge of providing clothing.

The men under this system enjoy free meals and unrestricted sex. There is one proviso for the latter, namely that although women are common property, if there are two men who want her (or if two women want one man), preference must first be given to the man or woman who is older and uglier. The children that result from the unions will be raised in common, and no one will know his or her own father. Under this system, older men are all treated as fathers, and younger males and females owe them respect.

In his edition and translation of this play, Alan Sommerstein says that Praxagora's society has been the 'basis for every subsequent communistically organised utopia in the western philosophical and political tradition.'[10] I am sure he is simply referring to the abolition of private property, since the regulation of sex would be difficult to enforce and the dependence on slaves for the smooth running of society is utterly impractical. Will there be enough slaves to fill all those needs? Won't wars be necessary either to defend the city or to replenish the supply of slaves as Greece usually did? Since the men are partying, who will conduct the wars? Who will do the actual fighting? Training slaves to be soldiers while the citizens' feast might soon lead to a change in government.

Aristophanes was writing something to amuse an Athenian audience, somewhat depressed in those years following Athens' defeat by Sparta. In the Athens of 392 BC, dominated by recession, any idea of caring women running the government while the men sat idly by all day was a wild fantasy. But wild fantasies were Aristophanic specialties.

Aristophanes' play enacts one of men's worst nightmares, namely women in power. The repression of women may have changed somewhat in the modern world, but there are still many people who see a clear danger in sharing power with women.

This is a play that shows a society primarily concerned about daily needs, particularly food and sex (not necessarily in that order). It makes little allowance for other drives in human nature, such as the desire to create, and possibly even to work, and to enjoy the fruits of one's work, and privacy: no one here has a private house from which he or she can bar strangers. There is some obvious need for public officers to supervise the running of the society.

Many could complain that there was still a lot to be explained and debated. But this is a comedy, not a legal constitution or a philosophical treatise. Philosophy is different. Plato, who could be called the father of western philosophy, came up with his own proposal for the ideal state. Plato's *Republic* tries to provide a model for a society in which humans could lead good and happy lives.

Plato's *Republic* takes much from earlier literary models. He suggests having leaders who are wise and educated, philosophers in fact, who make decisions for the rest with no regard for self-gain. Because of their own enlightenment, education and natural proclivities, they do not crave power, nor are they subject to greed because society provides for them. They have learned the benefits of moderation and practise the motto attributed to Solon carved on the temple at Delphi that says, 'Nothing in excess'.

Plato organises his ideal state with three classes of people: guardians who supply two of those classes – rulers to govern the state, and warriors to defend it – and workers, both skilled and unskilled, who provide for its physical needs. He banishes the poets and artists whom he claims misrepresent the truth and encourage the expression of excessive emotions unsuitable for the populace at large.

Everyone should practise what he or she does best and, from an early age, people are trained in their respective skills. Women are not excluded from any category. The guardians lead lives similar to those described in *Ecclesiazusae*, in that they have their needs met, but they certainly do not spend their days revelling at parties, and their sexuality is rigorously controlled. The warriors are there for defensive, not imperialist, purposes.

Property is supervised by the guardians and distributed according to the needs of each. There are regular 'sexual festivals' in which mating occurs, and somehow the guardians arrange that they mate only with other guardians.

Virtue governs this society with justice at the top. The first definition of justice is the proper differentiation of things: everything in its proper place and functioning well. A second definition includes fair treatment for all. Justice applies to all the classes, as does temperance or moderation, and control of baser impulses. Wisdom is the virtue that characterises the guardians who rule, and bravery characterises the warriors.

This all works smoothly if the ruler or rulers have indeed apprehended the truth about which Plato informs us in his cave analogy. He says that most of us are in a cave tied to chairs that face a wall on which we see only shadows of 'puppets' that are lit from behind. We see mere reflections of the truth. What happens when one person is dragged out of the cave into the sunlight and sees for the first time the brilliance of truth in all its splendour? The sight is painful, but when he grows accustomed to it, he is reluctant to go back to his former condition. He realises how most people are victims of illusion. He could choose to stay and contemplate the sun of reality, but his noble instincts finally prevail and he returns to teach other men. He is the ideal philosopher king.

One of the important points of Plato's cave parable is that truth is blinding and needs to be introduced gradually; otherwise the process will be very painful. Plato advises that teaching mathematics is of enormous help in preparing a person for the quest of truth.

Early in the *Republic*, Thrasymachus, a famous teacher of rhetoric, makes a case for the powerful doing what they want and securing what they perceive as good for themselves with no consideration for the good of others. Glaucon tells the myth of Gyges (King of Lydia). Gyges found a ring, which could make him invisible. The claim is that if anyone could make himself invisible, he would not hesitate to take all that he wants for himself with impunity: stealing property (including other men's wives), and literally getting away with murder. Glaucon contrasts the happiness of a truly good man who suffers slanders and torture against the happiness of this bad man who knows how to generate a good reputation and has amassed power and wealth for himself. Some philosophers claim that this argument has never been adequately refuted, namely that a successful life based on doing evil can bring more happiness to someone rather than one based on doing good if he must suffer for it. Plato would claim that a good man is happier, no matter what happens to him, because he knows the value of *true* happiness, one that no externals can touch; the man who commits evil, only *thinks* he is happy, and usually very briefly because that happiness depends on constant external needs being met. If one looks closely, it is seen that he lives with greed, desire, and fears that torture him internally. However, there are still many Glaucons in the world who, if pressed, would defend their way of life.

In book eight of the *Republic*, Plato presents different political systems and shows how one develops into the next. He thinks the best political system is his republic described above, in which the people all do what they are best suited for and are ruled and defended by enlightened guardians.

After that comes a timocracy, a government in which people try to surpass each other to gain fame and honour for their actions. This turns into an oligarchy based on wealth; winning honour cedes to acquiring power through wealth. Democracy is the next stage, as the lower classes grow more envious of the wealthy. Democracy for Plato was the society that put Socrates to death. In that system, no qualifications are needed for people in power; in fact, intelligence or any exceptional skills are regarded with suspicion. Education is mistrusted in all the systems except Plato's republic. In a democracy, all that is needed is the professed love of the people.

Plato sees this system as a type of anarchy driven by crude desires. Work is forgotten; leaders come and go and rise to power by persuasion of the masses rather than ability; factions are constantly quarrelling; the state eventually goes bankrupt from the chaos, and is ripe for a takeover by a tyrant. The people at first elect a man to restore order, but then he secures his power by the military and destroys his opposition. He kills the wealthy and seizes their property. Finally he even oppresses the very masses that gave him power. Plato sees this as the worst system of all. Yet this system still dominates today in so many places!

Plato's ideal republic looks better and better by comparison with these systems. In his republic, not only can people perform the jobs for which they are most suited, but there are also none of the struggles, which are associated with private property and the inequities which often result from this system because property is shared. Equality of women and the lack of an imperialist philosophy that advocates continual war for economic reasons are further benefits that contribute to the well-being of the people. In other systems, educated and ethical leaders may appear from time to time, but in Plato's republic this would be the rule rather than the exception.

There are still problems. The instinct to lay claim to one's own territory and property can be found in most animals, and it is difficult to eradicate in humans. Plato might object that it's only a question of education: getting the man who has seen only shadows finally to walk in the sunlight and see what is real.

Hypothetically, goods can be shared and distributed equitably, but sharing a wife, lover or child can be more problematic. This form of eugenics also limited the freedom of the citizens and could lead to the *dystopias* as envisioned by Aldous Huxley and George Orwell.

Plato's republic needs to incorporate more personal and emotional pleasures to be viable for most people. In addition to quality, life needs joy.

Plato might claim that Aristophanes' political system was a communist anarchy, driven by the base desires described in his picture of democracy. Certainly Plato's description of democracy reflects his Athens during the last days of the Peloponnesian War, and then the chaotic period after that. As predicted in the *Republic*, later in the fourth century Greek democracy was to degenerate into tyranny when Philip II, the king of Macedonia, and subsequently his son, Alexander the Great, assumed power.

The Roman republic has a legendary founding date of 510 BC (the same year as the overthrow of the Pisistratid tyranny and the birth of democracy in Athens). The Roman republic at first was aristocratic, with Patricians enjoying power, which was reluctantly shared with the Plebeians. Gradually the nobles had to cede power, and laws were codified in the Twelve Tables. The transition was handled well and the smooth running of their affairs allowed the Romans to conquer and consolidate Italy. Gradually their power extended beyond Italy and across the seas. The history of Rome was to a great extent a history of its wars. Factional fighting began soon after 133 BC, and continued until in 49 BC Julius Caesar crossed the Rubicon and marched on Rome; then the end of the republic was near. Following Caesar's assassination in 44, and the defeat of Mark Anthony at Actium in 31 BC, Octavian, Caesar's grand-nephew and adopted son, was left in charge and this signalled the definitive end of the republic. From Augustus (formerly Octavian) in 27 BC, to Constantine in 337 AD, emperors ruled Rome.

Utopias and dystopias vie for their ultimate visions from the Greeks to moderns. Human variability guarantees that there are no easy answers. The only thing we can count on is change.

Some of Plato's vision as articulated in his *Republic* has yet to be surpassed, and we can thank Aristophanes for making the first rough sketch. Plato added ethics. Social justice is still a goal rarely reached, but sorely needed at this present time.

The whole concept of ethics driving politics is something modern day politicians have to learn. Plato has well outlined how the seeds of rot can destroy the most powerful empire. Plato's *Republic* should be required reading for the leaders of the world, particularly those who have mastered the rhetoric of goodness and justice, without the reality to back it up. Too many politicians wear the ring of Gyges as they continue to amass power and wealth at the expense of ethics, and ultimately of the very people they should be serving.

I

Reclaiming the Republican Tradition

Iseult Honohan

1 What is republicanism?

Even now, when innovation and creativity have been award-ed an almost sacred status in society, the extent to which political actors feel the need to claim their place in a tradi-tion – presumably so that some of the sheen of illustrious pre-decessors will rub off on them – is striking. But traditions also embody norms that transcend current interpretations and immediate utility, and can be used to call to account those who claim to represent the tradition.

What it means to be a republican is a contested matter. This is true in Ireland, where republicanism has been asso-ciated with physical force separatism and cultural national-ism, as well as with a certain revolutionary austerity and authoritarianism. These reflect its genesis in eighteenth cen-tury movements that included revolutionaries as diverse as Jefferson and Robespierre, its growth in the age of European nationalism, and the influence of authoritarian catholicism on its constitutional expression.

But the republican tradition has broader foundations and a longer history than any one of these.

To begin with, republicanism is best understood not as requiring *national* independence or the absence of a monarch *per se*, but as opposing domination whether by external or internal forces, by government, individuals or sectional groups. Put more positively, it advocates realising freedom and self-government among citizens. The idea is that if those who are mutually vulnerable recognise that they share a common fate and can act in solidarity, they may jointly be able to exercise some collective direction over their lives.[1]

We might expect that a tradition that includes Machiavelli, John Milton, Oliver Cromwell, Mary Wollstonecraft, Ned Kelly, Michael McDowell and Gerry Adams – all self-styled republicans – has to be pretty heterogeneous – and it is. So, if there is a republican tradition, it consists not of a single thread but of multiple interwoven strands – Italian, English, Dutch, American, French and Australian to name a few – each with a different twist; there have been catholic, protestant, militantly secularist, radical and conservative, small city-state and extensive territorial republics.

But all these strands of republicanism seem to respond to the ineluctable interdependence of human beings, and the way in which their survival and flourishing depends on the kinds of social frameworks they inhabit. The political question with which republicans are concerned is what kind of *freedom* is possible in the light of this interdependence, and how it may be realised. This freedom is understood as a political achievement, rather than a natural possession of individuals. It is inherently fragile, and requires both a strong legal framework to prevent domination, and also the civic engagement of citizens in supporting the common goods they share, alongside their separate and often conflicting interests. Citizenship entails responsibilities as well as rights; and what self-governing citizens achieve is the chance to exercise some collective direction over their lives, rather than complete self-sufficiency. But common interests are easier to overlook, and therefore more vulnerable than individual interests; this gives rise to corruption – that is, pursuing individual or sectional interests at the expense of the common good. Corruption and domination are identified as the crucial political problems that have to be addressed. Freedom requires political equality and two dimensions of engaged, or active citizenship: public spirit, traditionally termed 'civic virtue', and political participation in determining what is in the common good. Thus republicanism offers an alternative to both the liberal emphasis on individual freedom and the communitarian emphasis on *pre*-political shared values or identity among citizens.

2 What is the tradition?

All political traditions are constituted or reconstituted in retrospect. And republicans have been perhaps the most self-consciously historical of all political thinkers, in seeing them-

selves as the inheritors of the political practices and authors
of classical Greece and Rome, notably Aristotle and Cicero.
The word 'republic' itself comes to us from the Latin *res publica*,
the 'public thing' or public concern, and the idea of freedom
as a legally guaranteed status is also a Roman legacy.

Republicanism first crystallised in early modern Europe
and its colonies. Its leading exponents, Machiavelli, Harrington, Rousseau and Madison, were not armchair theorists en-
gaging in utopian speculation; they addressed immediate political problems of the self-governing Florentine city-state, the
seventeenth century English republic (or commonwealth – the
first English translation of *res publica*), France, and the American colonies respectively. They articulated theories that reflected wider and often more turbulent public exchanges. All
defended the legitimacy and practicability of citizen self-
government against the concentrated power wielded by the
Medici family, Stuart and Bourbon kings and the metropolitan government in London, and they rejected the theoretical defences of sovereign power offered by Hobbes, among
others.[2] Their writings inspired two of the great modern revolutions in America and France.

So though the very existence and continuity of a republican tradition has often been challenged, and the place of
almost any figure you can name contested (Machiavelli is
better known as the author of *The Prince*, surely an advocate
of central power politics, Rousseau as the theorist of natural
rights and social contract, or general will, and so on). But,
however differently they frame their arguments, republican

theorists agree on a cluster of values: freedom, participation in self-government and commitment to the common good.

The core elements of the classical republican tradition that grew between the sixteenth and eighteenth centuries were first, a preference for forms of 'mixed government', neither wholly democratic nor monopolised by a sovereign. This creates a balance of social forces or institutions to prevent domination by particular corrupt interests and to realise the common good of citizens. Secondly, freedom is guaranteed by the rule of established laws, in place of the arbitrary will of a ruler; in Harrington's words this represents 'the empire of laws and not of men' under which citizens are free not *from* the law but *by* the law'.[3]

Preserving this fragile freedom from the threat of external and internal power depends thirdly, not only on good institutions, but also on developing the character of citizens with a strong commitment to the common good. For Machiavelli, citizens who 'neither arrogantly dominate nor humbly serve' must be active, accept duties and perform both political and military service.[4] Most republicans advocated a civic militia, both to provide defence and to instil civic spirit; this was one of Machiavelli's pet projects when he was secretary of the Florentine republic. (Its ironic legacy nowadays is found in the USA in the constitutional right – originally the duty – to bear arms.) For the less militaristic Rousseau, still 'the better the state is constituted, the more does public business takes precedence in the minds of the citizens' who should 'fly to the assembly'.[5] Since people will always experience tension between their individual and their common interests, some form of civic education is essential. Finally, substantial economic inequalities pose an obstacle to equal citizenship, citizens need to be independent of the overbearing will of others – in the terms of the time, this implied that they should be property owners. While some envisaged measures to limit excessive accumulation of wealth, it was more usual to exclude from citizenship those seen as naturally dependent: property-less wage-earners and women (though, it must be said that in this respect republicans were no different from 'early' liberals).

A kaleidoscope of different permutations of these ideas presented itself by the late eighteenth century, including many hybrids incorporating (more or less consistently) the newer idea of inalienable natural rights. This is the context in which the United Irishmen, following American and French example, called for the end of tyrannical rule in Ireland. Two strands in particular were important. In America James Madison, extended the theory to fit a large, increasingly commercial society. Co-author of the Federalist Papers and the US constitution, he boldly redefined a republic as government through representatives (as opposed to the direct popular rule of a democracy), and introduced separation of powers between federal and state governments as well as between branches of government. But it is less often noticed that he still emphasised the need for civic virtue in citizens and rulers: 'If there be no virtue we are in a wretched situation ... No theoretical checks, no form of government can render us secure.'[6]

A wholly different tack was taken by Rousseau who re-stated the idea that republican freedom was possible only in a small participatory community; though he did not hold out much hope that this could be realised anywhere in the modern world (with the possible exception of Corsica). But he deli-vered a swingeing criticism of the oppression and corruption of his time. This inspired the French revolutionaries to create a large republic based on the values of liberty, equality and fraternity, and to try to realise his elusive vision of the collec-tive sovereignty of the people (where 'each individual while uniting himself with others obeys no one but himself and re-mains as free as before').[7] At this time, though less influenti-ally, women writers, including Mary Wollstonecraft, expressed republican hopes for the improvement of society through self-rule and civic virtue to include women as equal citizens.[8]

Partly because it was discredited by the excesses of the French revolutionary terror, republicanism in the nine-teenth century was eclipsed by the more prominent move-ments of liberalism, socialism and nationalism. But it passed on significant legacies to each of these – ideas of balanced government and the rule of law to liberals, of social interde-pendence and the negative political effects of economic in-equality to socialists, and of collective self-government to nationalists. It also had an interesting, if largely overlooked, afterlife in the work of those archetypal liberals, Constant, Tocqueville and Mill – all of whom stressed (as well as free-dom) the importance of active citizens concerned with the wider good of society.

But even as the vote was gradually extended to the working-class and to women, the idea of active participation was sidelined, seen as dangerous or impractical. And civic virtue was increasingly seen as redundant in commercial societies. So citizenship became broader at the cost of becoming shallower. As one writer neatly sums it up, the civic, political and urban ideal was succeeded by one that was civil, polite and urbane.[9]

Contemporary liberal democracies have almost all been shaped to some extent by the institutional example of the American and French revolutions. But few countries are as consciously republican as France, where the idea of the 'republic' plays an explicit normative role, and economic, social and education policies, for example, are regularly justified and opposed in terms of their republican origins and credentials – with a distinctive emphasis on rationality, uniformity and secularity or *laïcite*, expounded in official republican manuals to educate citizens, most recently the *Guide Républicain*, widely distributed in the summer of 2004 in the aftermath of the latest headscarf controversy.[10]

Irish republicanism has had a tendency to focus narrowly on national independence and the military means to achieve this, rather than the freedom or participation of individual citizens. The republic established under de Valera exemplified a more communitarian and authoritarian republicanism. It aimed to realise not a politically determined common good based on deliberative participation, but a pre-politically defined vision of the good for society that was shaped by cultural nationalism and a powerful institutional church.[11]

Thus republican ideas have had different practical legacies, each coloured by the particular context in which they developed.

3. *Why has it been revived and why is it worth reclaiming?*
Although liberalism had a sweeping victory over socialism in the global realignment of the 1990s, there has since then been a remarkable revival of republican ideas. This seems to stem from an increasing sense that, if liberalism is all there is, there is something missing. We might look briefly at four concerns that have emerged, namely, the limits of market freedom; a democratic deficit; fragmentation and declining social responsibility; and the identification of citizenship with national culture. While more communitarian reactions call for the renewal of moral or religious purpose and community in politics, I will suggest that republicanism has a distinctive approach, and offers resources to address these concerns in its approach to *freedom, political participation, solidarity and the basis for citizenship in interdependence*.

a. Freedom
Since the Thatcher and Reagan years a particular view of freedom has been dominant in public policy discourse. In this (neo-liberal) view freedom is possessed by individuals to the extent that they are not interfered with, and the principal threat to that freedom is government; thus freedom is promoted if government activity is reduced to the minimum,

by privatising and deregulating, paring down or contracting out public services, and above all, cutting taxation and increasing individual disposable income. But this is too limited an account of freedom; it overlooks threats to freedom that do not come from the state, but from individuals or groups that can exercise arbitrary or unaccountable power: e.g. established elites in religious or cultural communities, corporations who endanger the health of their workers and consumers, and media cartels who control the news available to the public.

Thus stronger government intervention may be needed to promote freedom by providing secure guarantees against such arbitrary domination, wherever it may arise. And maintaining the equal status of citizens may depend on government measures to limit the effects of economic and social inequality on political status by supplying the material *conditions* for the exercise of freedom.

b. Participation

Second, there has been much discussion of the problem of political apathy, measured in decline in voter turn-out in almost all democracies today. This reflects a widespread feeling of powerlessness and alienation from politics, and a sense that citizenship lacks depth and meaning, that significant questions are either not publicly debated, or that people's voices are not heard. The republican valuation of participation in politics calls for more opportunities and structured public spaces for ordinary people to contribute to political decisions – not just to express individual or sectional interests more effectively, but to encourage deliberation about the common interests shared by otherwise diverse citizens. As Hannah Pitkin put it, 'what distinguishes public life is the potential for decisions to be made ... actually by the community collectively, through participatory public action and in the common interest ... the possibility of a shared collective, deliberate, active intervention in our fate, in what otherwise would be the by-product of private decisions.'[12] While it is true, as Madison noted, that 'the room will not hold all', critics of such expanded participation as impractical due to numbers or competence overlook the possibilities of multi-level institutions. These are being experimented with – from local and regional to trans-national levels: citizens' juries, deliberative polling, participatory budgets. And, in the light of contemporary scandals, the contrast between passionate, ignorant and sectionally interested citizens and rational, informed and disinterested representatives may well seem overdrawn.

The point of this is not to make participation compulsory, but to offer more opportunities for people to have a say in things that affect them directly, and to elicit more deliberative engagement with other viewpoints when they do participate.

c. Common goods

A third concern that has surfaced in post-Celtic Tiger Ireland is that the sense of community and social concern that was a feature of an older (if in other ways poorer) Ireland is in danger of being eroded. The great increase in private wealth and prosperity seems to have been accompanied by more fragmentation and isolation, and declining social responsibility – notably among the more prosperous and privileged.

In politics we have seen revelations of corruption, not just among a few individuals, but pervasive practices undermining the public interest in good planning and equal application of taxation.

While the role of markets in expanding wealth is now indisputable, there is a risk that those common goods – our cultural and environmental heritage, health and social provision (things that cannot be secured by the market) will be overlooked; the phrase 'public wealth and private squalor' coined by Galbraith to describe 1950s America evokes more than a glint of recognition in contemporary Ireland.[13]

There has to be a significant role for the state in securing these goods. But that in turn depends on the recognition by citizens that they do share common goods, and on their willingness to accept certain limits on their pursuit of private interests. Equally, while legal procedures for greater accountability are essential to prevent corruption, volumes of ethics legislation and strings of inquiries will not safeguard the common good if there is no sense of common concerns among citizens.

We should be wary of exhortations to be more active or civic spirited, or to join voluntary associations in order to strengthen social capital, unless ordinary citizens are given a larger voice in decision-making, opportunities for meaningful participation and the material conditions necessary for freedom. The language of the common good can be used hypocritically, and the greater the inequalities between citizens, the less we can talk about 'common' rather than 'club' goods – that is, publicly supported goods that benefit only those with the capacities, time and resources to avail of them.

d. The basis of citizenship

The final concern I will point to is the way in which a link between citizenship (and its commitments) and ethnic or cultural identity can be arbitrarily exclusive or oppressive.

In the view of many, the nation-state cannot unproblematically be the unit of self-government today, because nations are too large for self-government and too small to challenge the power of multinationals and to deal with global problems of the environment and security. Moreover, historical vicissitudes and ever increasing mobility mean that few countries are nationally homogeneous today, so that linking cultural identity and citizenship is likely to lead to conflict or oppression of minorities. But national identity seems to be an increasingly powerful political force, as seen dramatically in Eastern Europe after the overthrow of socialism. And, elsewhere in the so-called west, after a period of multicultural accommodation, there seems to be a new demand for national or cultural commonality among citizens – sometimes based on the idea that, for example, the support of citizens for distributive welfare measures requires this. In the context of increasing immigration, this view has given rise to proposals for more stringent requirements for admission and requirements of cultural assimilation as a condition of citizenship.

From a republican perspective the grounds for civic virtue and solidarity among citizens are seen as relying on the recognition of interdependence rather than ethnic commonality or cultural identity. The term patriotism originally conveyed a commitment to the common good of the community, contrasted not to other nations, but to the self-interest of individuals or sectional groups. The republican argument is that solidarity can be generated through interaction among citizens. Perhaps national identity has been a substitute for participation in giving a sense of belonging, but it does not necessarily generate commitment. The fact that someone cheers for the Irish soccer team does not necessarily mean that they show any concrete solidarity with other citizens.

A political community is composed of people who do not necessarily share a common culture, but who find themselves together, sharing a wide range of interrelated interdependencies framed by the political institutions to which they are subject, and who have some possibility of collectively shaping their future. This grounds membership in the interdependence and mutual vulnerability of people who share a common fate. The difference between citizenship as cultural identity and citizenship as shared fate was well expressed by Ireland's first muslim TD, Mosajee Bhamjee when he said in an interview, 'I am an Irish citizen – of course in one way I will never be Irish, but I will *die* in Ireland'.[14]

In rooting citizenship in the interdependence and mutual vulnerability of those who share a common fate and future, a republican account of citizenship is at least potentially more open than those based on than common ethnicity or culture. This favours relatively generous conditions of naturalisation (and dual citizenship). It also suggests that, even if some measures needed to be taken to remove perverse incentives for people to give birth in Ireland, the balance of citizenship should not so lightly have been tilted towards *ius sanguinis* (based on descent) from *ius soli* (based on place of birth, if we can take that as a predictor of a common future), as it was in the 2004 citizenship referendum. Moreover, although membership is always bounded, citizenship can be more porous and accommodating and more open to develop at multiple levels – possibly up to the global – than if it is culturally or ethnically defined.

4. Conclusion

Republicanism went into abeyance with the development of the sovereign nation-state that accommodated the growth of commerce and populations. If factors such as economic globalisation and environmental risk now reduce the appropriateness of the nation-state as the basis of political community, alternative ways of organising our political life may need to be considered. Republicanism, a tradition that was sidelined, may have something to offer now that conditions have changed again.

But the emphasis on common goods and civic virtue, and

the ways in which these were formulated have led to charges that republicanism is inherently oppressive, moralistic, exclusive, militarist and masculinist. Any contemporary rearticulation of the theory has to overcome these objections.

But we may understand the emphasis on the common good as setting standards for all of our public lives, and encouraging commitment to the wider good as a horizon of concern, and not as imposing a particular, fixed conception of the common good, or a moral code for every aspect of life. Thus it does not imply reverting to an authoritarian and moralistic community.

Republicanism *has* taken authoritarian, militaristic and sectarian forms both in theory and practice. We would do better to show how these are subject to internal criticism in terms of domination than to dismiss republicanism on that account, thus throwing out the collective and participatory baby with the authoritarian bathwater.

It is worth emphasising that republicanism is not so much diametrically opposed to liberalism, as an older tradition that has contributed to its development in the past, and may now represent a valuable corrective to the prevailing account of liberalism, with its emphasis on legal rights and safeguards, and a narrow account of freedom as the absence of interference (mainly by the state).

It is not opposed to liberalism's central value of liberty, but has a different centre of gravity within a cluster of values of liberty, participation in self-government and solidarity. It is the conjunction of freedom with these other concerns of civic engagement that is characteristic of republicanism. The hope is that citizenship might be able to become more substantial without becoming narrower. But this is a theory still under development rather than one ready made for application to contemporary concerns.

2

Theobald Wolfe Tone and Irish Republicanism and Separatism[1]

Thomas Bartlett

Was Wolfe Tone a republican? Was he a separatist? At one time for an Irish historian to have posed such a question was to run the risk of being labelled 'revisionist', accused of wilfulness and denounced as anti-national. Tone's separatism and republicanism seemed to be so much a matter of historical record that probing them could scarcely be seen as anything other than redundant, impertinent or even perverse. After all he had claimed that his objects had been to:

> subvert the tyranny of our execrable government, to break the connection with England, the never-failing source of all our political evils and to assert the independence of my country

and in his speech at his court martial, he had averred:

> from my earliest youth I have regarded the connection between Ireland and Great Britain as the curse of the Irish nation; and

> felt convinced that whilst it lasted, this country could never be free nor happy.

Statements such as these had spoken out so apparently categorically that all further discussion appeared unnecessary.

However, Tone's assertion of a life-long commitment to separatism has received short shrift from his most recent biographers. One tartly rebutted this claim by stating that 'the facts furnish all the comment that is necessary' and this view was later amplified by another who cast Tone as an unanchored misfit, an 'outsider', who longed to find 'an acceptable career, a meaningful role, some fulfilment of the expectations natural to a member of the colonial elite', and who, through 'alienation and despair' became a separatist and a revolutionary.[2] A third biographer has claimed that Tone's conversion to separatism was almost wholly a product of his American exile and was thus not only comparatively late in the day, but represented 'a case of necessity as much as choice', and was even 'an accident of character as much as of timing'.[3] Moreover, Tone's scattered references to the 'New Ireland' that would be brought about once French victory had severed the link, have suggested to some writers that he was prepared to envisage not so much an Ireland independent, separate and free, but rather a French military colony – a sort of Hibernian republic, sister-satellite to the Batavian republic – in which there would be laws restricting press freedom, and in which the existing social order (and distribution of property) would be safeguarded:

'The very same laws which under the English constitution I regard as tyrannical and unjust', Tone noted complacently, 'I would in a free republic preserve and even strengthen'.

As with Tone's separatism, so too his republican credentials have been called into question. There was Tone's enthusiasm for colonial enterprises in the South Seas, his unabashed admiration for French aggression, his loathing of the new American republic, even his fondness and sympathy for both George III and Louis XVI. Such attitudes hardly seem in keeping with the common perception of true republican principles. Again, we may note Tone's lack of interest in cultural matters – Irish music, history, language and literature left him cold; while his patronising attitude towards catholics in general, but towards especially 'Poor Pat', the prisoner of war, easily bought for a bottle of wine and a tumble with a *fille de joie*, has been emphasised.[4] Tone, remarks one commentator, may have turned his back on the protestant ascendancy, but he did not – could not? – reject the outlook of easy cultural superiority that was inseparable from it.

Finally, Tone's biographers have in general been at pains to stress that his ideas (and he was not a systematic thinker) contained little that was unconventional. His *Argument*, for example, 'said nothing new and owed much to ideas then in general circulation'; and there was little that was novel in those other notions linked to his name. The necessity for a strategic alliance with catholics in order to pursue parliamentary reform had been clear since the early 1780s. The desirability of a drastic reduction of English influence in Irish affairs had likewise been a common aspiration long before Tone came on the political scene, and even Tone's complaints about the poor figure Ireland cut in international affairs had been anticipated by Sir Laurence Parsons and others.

All in all, it has been suggested that Tone was largely marginal to the 1790s: he was *not* the founder of the United Irishmen, *not* the architect of the French alliance, *not* the sole United Irish representative in Paris, *not* a player in the 1798 rebellion. Nor, for that matter, was he marginal only to the 1790s, for it has been further argued that for most of the nineteenth century Tone languished in comparative neglect until he was taken up, as it were from obscurity, by Patrick Pearse in 1913 and declared to be, 'the greatest of Irish nationalists ... the greatest of Irishmen'.

The elements of adventurism, giddiness, militarism and even opportunism in his make-up have been stressed by his most recent biographer:

> Not having been a revolutionary before 1795, when pushed into becoming one, he responded with all the zeal of the convert. But it was a single-mindedness that could just as easily propel Tone in one direction as another, and one may query his having emerged as a revolutionary had it not been for the exceptional nature of the times in which he lived.[5]

Such provocative insights invite a further reflection on Tone's thought and achievements: it may be found on examination that his claim to novelty, as well as consistency, are rather stronger than has been maintained.

At the outset, it is clear that Tone's republicanism must

be firmly located in the eighteenth century, and judged by the criteria of the time, rather than by the standards of later generations. But when we come to define what was meant by republicanism at that period, we find that there was little agreement even among 'republicans' on the central elements of their creed. Tom Paine, involved in the American, French – and Irish – revolutions, noted that 'it has always been the political craft of courtiers and court government to abuse something which they call republicanism: but what that republicanism was or is they never attempt to explain'.

However, it could be claimed that republicans had only themselves to blame for these attacks, for they themselves were notoriously vague as to what they meant. No less a personage than one of the 'founding fathers' of American republicanism, John Adams, confessed in 1807 that he had 'never understood' what a republic was and 'no other man ever did or ever will'. Republicans espoused contrary views as to whether a republican form of government was suitable to a small country or to a large one. They disputed whether a republic would have a propensity for peace or for war (Machiavelli had appeared to argue both propositions). Contradictory viewpoints were voiced on the question of whether a republic should foster commerce or seek to restrain economic growth; and there was little agreement on such weighty matters as equality and representation. Nor indeed was there a consensus on the question of whether a republic had to adopt a specific form of government. Provided the 'common weal' was pursued, and 'commonwealth' was for a long time the usual translation from the latin *republica*, there was much scope for discussion.

'What the republicans take themselves to be describing', notes the political theorist, Quentin Skinner

> is any set of constitutional arrangements under which it might justifiably be claimed that the *res* (the government) genuinely reflects the will and promotes the good of the *publica* (the community as a whole). Whether a *res publica* has to take the form of a self-governing republic is not therefore an empty definitional question but rather a matter for earnest enquiry and debate.

Viewed in this light, it is clear that in the eighteenth century a republic was by no means incompatible with monarchy. Machiavelli, the republican and author of the *Discourses*, was also Machiavelli, the monarchist and author of *The Prince*, and the classic republican texts since then – those by Smith, Harrington and Sydney – had been equally ambivalent on this question.

Republicanism since the sixteenth century, writes J. G. A. Pocock, was 'more a language than a programme' and the vocabulary was one of protest, of resistance to tyrants, combining an obsession with corruption with a quest for civic virtue. It was generally assumed that political virtue and civic virtue would be found most readily, though not exclusively, in a country whose citizens had the predominant part in the election or selection of their magistrate, prince or king. For this reason, republicans everywhere sought to give a preponderant role to the people. Where the people had little or no say, either because of despotism or corruption, republicans were generally found to be seeking a return to some golden age or, more often, advocating parliamentary reform.

However, if there was little agreement among republicans on the precise form of republican government, there was universal recognition of the spirit which ought to infuse it. From Machiavelli to Paine and including Milton, Harrington, Montesquieu and Gibbon, republican writers agreed that 'public virtue is the only foundation of republics' (John Adams). This moral dimension to republicanism came before everything else: with it, the common good was promoted and liberty protected; without it, chaos and corruption reigned. Republicanism therefore constituted a moral challenge to its adherents, placing a heavy burden on them to live up to its promise.

Where does Tone stand in this brief examination of eighteenth-century republicanism? Tone never claimed to be an ideologue: he wrote

> I confess I dislike abstract reasoning on practical subjects. I am buried in matter. When I feel a grievance pinch me sorely I look neither for the major nor minor of a proposition or syllogism but merely for the proximate cause and the possibility of removing it.

As both Dunne and Elliott have noted, he was far from being a systematic thinker: Dunne even warns against any attempt 'at over-systematising the scattered polemics and autobiographical fragments addressed to different audiences for a variety of purposes by a young man who was more an activist than a thinker'; and Hubert Butler, in his elegant essay on

Tone, remarks that 'what made Tone great was that he had no ideology'.[6] That said, there are good grounds for arguing that Tone had been from an early date a thorough-going republican; at any rate, he was as much a republican as those whose credentials in that respect have never been questioned.

In the first instance, Tone's language was unmistakably republican, filled with notions of resistance to tyrants, opposition to hereditary aristocracies and replete with aspirations to end corruption and promote virtue. In these respects, we can see Tone's indebtedness to that eighteenth-century commonwealthman, or republican rhetoric, associated with Swift, Molesworth, Hutcheson and Toland. There existed in Dublin a republican coterie in the mid-eighteenth century which was vital in communicating commonwealthman ideas to a new generation. Tone's faith in parliamentary reform – 'with a parliament thus reformed everything is easy; without it nothing can be done' – was wholly republican and recognisably within the republican tradition. His social conservatism was equally in keeping with republican thought as it had developed since the renaissance. The references in his writings to the men of no property were few and far between (and were in any case ambiguous); and he grew indignant at the charge that the United Irishmen aimed at 'a distribution of property and an agrarian law'. Nor does Tone's preference for 'strong' government call into question his republicanism. His determination that while there would be 'just and reasonable liberty of the press', 'libels and calumnies' on the government would be severely punished was unexceptional, for libel laws – and sumptuary laws and price controls – were part of the republican agenda at that date. Equally, Tone's admiration for the martial virtues, even to the extent of proposing a military colony in the South Seas, should best be seen not as the negation of republicanism but (as Marianne Elliott reminds us) rather as evidence of 'a continuing mesmerisation with the military vigour of ancient Rome'.

So far as religion was concerned, Tone followed what could be called orthodox republican thought, though in doing so he parted company with Tom Paine who ridiculed religion. Tone was no friend to state-established religions but he believed that religion had a role to play in the republic. He was, like many of the classical republican writers, very hostile to the catholic church and the papacy and he saw republicanism with its emphasis on independence and virtue as the perfect antidote to clerical thraldom in Ireland and Europe. It may be argued that he especially admired the French revolution for its attack on the catholic church, the catholic clergy and ultimately on the pope himself. Even Tone's apparent sympathy for George III and Louis XVI ought to be seen as in keeping with republican ambivalence where monarchy was concerned, rather than as evidence of lukewarm commitment to republicanism itself. Tone's republicanism was certainly eclectic, but this was because republicanism was itself eclectic at that time. It is only when twentieth-century criteria of republicanism are applied to Tone that he is found wanting. Viewed amongst his contemporaries, Tone is seen for what he was – a recognisable eighteenth-century republican.

In a similar fashion, Tone's contribution to the modern separatist ideal – that Ireland could exist separate from Britain *and independent of all other countries* – may have been underestimated. Certainly, separatism, in the sense of merely severing the links with Britain, had been tossed around in Irish political discourse for several hundred years, but it had been very much a minority demand, typically voiced by religious exiles marooned on the continent. Much more common were the fervent declarations made by Irish 'rebels' of loyalty to the English crown and connection. In any case, rarely, if ever, until the late eighteenth century was it envisaged that Ireland could go it alone, for separation from England was commonly seen as a necessary prelude to connection with Spain or France.

Admittedly, some English politicians were convinced that they could hear the authentic separatist note in the rhetoric of the Anglo-Irish opposition spokesmen of the early and mid-eighteenth century. Dark rumours circulated during the party strife of the 1690s, the Wood's Halfpence controversy of the 1720s, and the Money Bill dispute of the 1750s that, in effect, the Anglo-Irish 'were foolishly and seditiously ... everyday aiming at independency'. Tone himself may have caught something of these fears when he wrote that his:

> 'great discovery', viz. that 'the influence of England was the radical vice of our government ... [and] ... that Ireland would

> never be either free, prosperous or happy ... whilst the connec-
> tion with England lasted'

could have been found in the works of Swift and Molyneux.
There was, of course, no hint of separatism in the writings of
these men: they were concerned to reform and thus strength-
en the link between Ireland and England, not endanger,
much less break it. However, Tone was correct in pointing
out that 'the bare mention of a doubt on the subject [i.e. the
connection between Ireland and England] had an instan-
taneous effect on the nerves of the English government'.

Not the least of the ironies to do with modern Irish
separatism is that its origins may be located in England.

Quite why English observers should have considered
separatism to be an element with Irish patriotism is something of a puzzle. Anxiety over the 'true' nature of the connection – was Ireland a colony, conquered province or sister
kingdom? – may have played a part here, and so too, surely,
did the English view of the Anglo-Irish relationship as being
identical to that between a mother and its child, with Ireland being cast in the role of dependent child. Implicit in
this child-colony/mother-country relationship was the threat
that the 'child' would one day grow up and seek independence and separation. Moreover, by the 1760s that day when
Ireland might seek independence did not appear to be all
that far off. It was still possible to claim in the 1740s that 'we
are come too late into the world to set up for ourselves', but
growing Irish prosperity, the apparent extinction of the cat-

holic menace, and the concurrent growth of protestant nationalism threatened to undermine Ireland's continuing subordination to England.

The secession of the American colonies, too, might prove
contagious, and it was surely in recognition of this threat
that from the 1770s on there emerged a distinct constitu-
ency in English politics which saw a legislative union, on
both financial and political grounds, as the ultimate solution
to the problem of Anglo-Irish relations. Unionism fed on the
fear of separation; and that fear, already heightened by the
winning of the 'Constitution of 1782', was further fuelled by
the failure in the 1780s to repair that dangerously flawed
'final settlement'. But unionism also bred separatism, for the
more talk there was of union, and the more that option was
couched in the Manichean terms of 'union or separation',
then the more the idea of separation came to be discussed.
Ironically, it was the arch-unionist, John Fitzgibbon, earl of
Clare, who did most to propagate the idea of separatism in
the 1780s through his scaremongering tactics during the
campaign for parliamentary reform and the regency crisis.
Years later, Tone impishly warned Clare that, 'stirring the
question' of separation might be unwise as 'public opinion is
an uncertain thing [and] ... it is therefore possible that the
investigation may not serve his side of the argument.'

Where does Tone stand in the separatist tradition? Clearly he did not invent the idea: English anxiety, the American
example, the growth of unionism and, latterly, Clare's in-
cautious pronouncements on the subject, had kept the matter

in the public domain. Moreover, separatism was, if not implicit, then concealed somewhere in the colonial nationalism espoused in Ireland in the eighteenth century. In any case, separatism as a political concept was in the air: when the American colonies had successfully claimed their independence, it had received its greatest boost since the setting up of the Dutch republic at the end of the sixteenth century. Nor can we accept Tone's claim made in France in 1796 that he was a separatist from his earliest days. That said, there was a separatist note to his writings, a separatist logic to his actions and a willingness to embrace the separatist option that together marked Tone out as the first Irish separatist.

Some years after publication, Tone claimed that in *Spanish War!* (1790), he had 'advanced the question of separatism with scarcely any reserve', though in fact overtly separatist sentiments were well concealed in this tract. Tone's demand for a national flag, navy and army could have been accommodated within the existing Anglo-Irish relationship. On the other hand, such appendages were the usual ones for fully sovereign states and it is clear that Tone was in effect, attempting to move the issue of national independence onto the agenda of Irish politics. But he moved very cautiously. In his *Argument* (1791), he started to answer those who claimed that 'Ireland is unable to exist as an independent state', but then apparently, he thought better of it:

> There is no one position, moral, physical or political that I hear with such extreme exacerbation of mind as this which denies to my country the possibility of independent existence.

It is not, however, my plan here to examine that question. I trust that when the necessity arises, as at some time it infallibly must, it will be found that we are as competent to our own government, regulation, and defence as any state in Europe. Till the emergency does occur it will but exasperate and inflame the minds of men to investigate and demonstrate the infinite resources and provocations to independence which every hour brings forth in Ireland. I shall therefore content myself with protesting on behalf of my country against the position as an infamous falsehood insulting to her pride and derogatory to her honour and I little doubt if occasion should arise but that I shall be able to prove it so.

Some months before the publication of the *Argument*, he had written to Russell his notorious letter in which he had admitted that as 'for separation ... I give it to you and your friends as my most decided opinion that such an event would be the regeneration to this country', but at the same time he admitted that 'that opinion is for the present too hardy'. Tone undoubtedly harboured separatist thoughts from an early date, but while he was prepared to contemplate the hitherto unthinkable, he still remained a reluctant separatist, and his advocacy of it was confined to private letters and conversations. It was John Fitzgibbon, earl of Clare who brought the separatist option, and Tone's espousal of it, into the open. Long convinced that the redoubt of the protestant ascendancy could never be captured by storm but only by betrayal, Fitzgibbon, from an early date, had his eye firmly on Tone, who seemed tailor-made for the role of traitor within the gate.

Ruthlessly, he used Tone's private letter of July 1791 to

Russell, time and time again, to denounce all United Irishmen as out and out separatists. In July 1793, Tone wrote to the editor of the *Freeman's Journal* protesting about Fitzgibbon's use, or misuse, of a private letter. Tone claimed that he was not a separatist. But his denial was hedged with so many conditions and qualifications as to be quite unconvincing. He accepted that the link could be 'highly beneficial' *provided* there was 'perfect equality, equal law, equal commerce, equal liberty [and] equal justice'; but so long as the 'gross corruption in the legislature' continued, so long as there was a 'sacrifice of [Ireland's] interests to England', then, claimed Tone, the separatist option – 'a question of weighty and serious import indeed' – would make advances:

> 'I for one do not wish to break that connection', he added piously, *'provided it can be*, as I am sure it can, preserved consistently with the honour, the interests and the happiness of Ireland. If I were, on the other hand, satisfied that it could not be so preserved, I would hold it a sacred duty to endeavour by all possible means to break it.'[7]

Even at this stage, Tone surely knew that the interests of Ireland would receive short shrift from England during the war; that after 1793 the only alternative, as Fitzgibbon never tired of declaring, was union or separation, not union or reform. Reform to Fitzgibbon and, increasingly, to British ministers was merely another word for separation. It was Tone's realisation that such was the case, that the republicanism which he sought could only be achieved through breaking the link, that drove him along the road to separation.

Other republicans, William Drennan, for example, re-sisted this logic and sought through their involvement in education and civic improvement to bring about that clas-sical republicanism which alone would 'save the nation'. Drennan, and others, shied away from from separatism be-cause they feared that the numerical superiority of Irish catholics, and indeed the very nature of Irish catholicism, might in fact prevent the realisation of republican ideals if Ireland were to be separated from England.

Tone, however, had been an activist on behalf of the catholics, had been persuaded that they had that necessary *capaces libertatis*, and was convinced that the perceived re-pellent aspects of Irish catholicism would wither away in a republican environment. In any case, the fall of the most catholic monarchy of France, and the flight of the pope him-self, gave grounds for re-assurance on that score. However, so long as the connection with England remained, Tone be-lieved that his republican ideals could not be realised. It was, in the end, he believed, English connection, not Irish division, that thwarted the achievement of republicanism: and the English connection had, therefore, to go.

3

The Easter Proclamation of 1916 and the Democratic Programme

Martin Mansergh

1916 was the great watershed in Irish history. 'All changed, changed utterly', was how Yeats set its significance in poetic stone. We view the proclamation and the rising against two backgrounds, what went before, and much that has happened since.

It achieved, like no other event, iconic status at the pinnacle of the republican tradition. Yet, what was dominant in the lead-up to the rebellion was more a separatist philosophy, from which a republic but also other constitutional models could have been derived.

Eoghan Roe O'Neill put forward an Irish republic to King Philip III of Spain in 1627, as a way of securing reconquest of lands and virtual independence under Spanish protection. When Wolfe Tone and the United Irishmen in the 1790s made a republic their objective, they had in mind the recent foundation of the United States, then only a small country, and the new French republic as the models most likely to win mass popular support. An Irish national democracy was their real objective, something deeply subversive to what was deludedly described by its champions as 'our glorious constitution'. It is worth remembering that the United Irishmen began as a constitutional organisation, which only went underground when all constitutional progress was blocked.

A generation later, Young Ireland sought virtual independence, without going deeply into the question of shared monarchy or a republic. 1848, and the tricolour brought home by Thomas Francis Meagher of 'the Sword' from revolutionary Paris marked the beginning of a transition to the next generation, the Fenians, whose secret and separatist organisation founded in 1858 was known as the Irish Republican Brotherhood. The Irish republic 'virtually established' in 1869 was the first shadowy construct of a parallel underground state.

As John O'Leary remarked, if Young Ireland had failed and failed definitely in her revolutionary policy, she had certainly not failed in her educating and propagandist policy. Much the same could be said of the Fenians. Freedom from foreign control mattered far more than forms of government. Indeed, the old Fenian, John Devoy, ended up backing the free state against the republic, or whatever put him on the opposite side to de Valera.

What made the Fenians more formidable was that they

were partly based across the ocean amidst the growing power of the United States, that had no affectionate memories of, or regard for, the British empire. The anticipated conflict between Britain and America, though it nearly occurred during the American Civil War, never came to pass. It was not until the First World War that 'England's difficulty' once again became 'Ireland's opportunity'.

That maxim dates from the late eighteenth century, as does the description that survives to this day of paramilitary forces as Volunteers, whether Irish or Ulster, loyalist or republican.

Charles Kickham, titular president and, through his novels and short stories, a voice of the people, idealised the temporary and flawed unity of traditions best exemplified by the Irish Volunteer Convention in Dungannon in 1782, which provided the armed backing that secured legislative independence. Despite the best efforts of Young Ireland to rally all traditions, Kickham recognised sadly that: 'When Freedom's sun rises over an enfranchised Irish nation, there will be no flag with Dungannon inscribed upon it lifted to the light'.

He recognised that reconciliation was simply not possible, until both domination and subjection were brought to an end.

The Act of Union of 1800 was an attempt by William Pitt by agreement with an unrepresentative and partially corrupt élite to pre-empt Irish democracy by abolishing the Irish parliament and thereby secure Britain's strategic flank in the midst of the revolutionary wars with France. After the

Irish revolution was defeated in 1798 and finally in 1803, pro-gressive-minded people attached to their country had little choice but to accept a pace of change that would be piece-meal and reformist. The liberal element in northern protes-tantism was largely satisfied with this and, with some noted exceptions, eventually merged into Ulster unionism.

Over the course of more than a century, the monopolies of power and wealth, that served as bastions of the British con-nection, were gradually worn away. This was done by a com-bination of parliamentary action in alliance with progressive British political forces, agitation, constitutional and other-wise, and charismatic leadership, against a background of spo-radic acts of violence, both political and agrarian. Achieve-ments included catholic emancipation; the abolition of tithes and later disestablishment; catholic university education; land reform and purchase; and parliamentary and local govern-ment reform.

Physical force or advanced nationalism was not central to most of these struggles. But, when they did join the Irish Parliamentary Party and the Land League in 1878 in the 'New Departure', a model for the democratic nationalist con-sensus in the early stages of the peace process, a tremendous impetus was given to a transformation of land ownership and towards bringing Ireland within a few years to the threshold of home rule. Unfortunately, it was not able to progress further past the obstacle of the house of lords veto.

The cultural revival was a final and culminating element in challenging British hegemony in Ireland, summed up in the title of Douglas Hyde's famous lecture in 1892, 'On the necessity of de-anglicising Ireland', which was seminal in the foundation of the Gaelic League. Whether in the context of home rule or independence, a distinct Irish nationality, denied or belittled by unionists, would be underpinned by a revival of the language, of native customs, traditions, sports and the evocation of the 'historic Irish nation', of an Ireland prior to the flight of the earls in 1607. In economic terms, there was a conviction that Ireland was capable of being, and ought to be, much more self-sufficient, with the spread of agricultural co-operatives providing a demonstration model.

In none of these debates that permeated the 1890s and the first decade and a half of the twentieth century, did the republic or republicanism feature very much. But the rhetoric of the centenary in 1898 of the 1798 Rebellion and advanced nationalist support for the Boer republics in the South African war were the harbinger of a steely and tough-minded determination to win Irish freedom in the coming generation by whatever means. Sinn Féin, founded by Arthur Griffith in 1905, advocated a revived and strengthened 1782 parliament operating on the model of the dual Austro-Hungarian monarchy, in other words, complete internal independence created by the abstention of Irish members from Westminster and their reconstitution as a national assembly.

Even Pearse was initially ready to embrace political and cultural autonomy by instalment, and he did much research on dual culture countries such as Belgium. What no nationalist of any persuasion was prepared to contemplate was that ongoing unionist obstruction and defiance in blocking home rule would be allowed to be successful, even when it had to resort to extra-legal means. Still less palatable in 1914 was the looming alternative of 'temporary', then permanent, partition and the loss of most of the economically rich province of Ulster where the 'historic Irish nation' had been most strongly concentrated, as the eventual price of a diluted home rule put on the long finger. As Desmond FitzGerald, a publicist in the war of independence and later a free state minister, put it in his memoirs, 'it is undignified for a nation to confine itself to purely constitutional action in the parliament of their overlords', especially when forty years of constitutional action 'was cancelled by the fact that the men in the north had armed'.

Ironically, from the 1860s to 1914, it was the protestant Ulstermen who were regularly depicted by newspapermen such as Walter Bagehot and Lord Northcliffe as the Prussians of Ireland, who would not hesitate to resort to arms, whereas Irish nationalists were written off, as Matthew Arnold depicted them, as impractical, romantic dreamers. In 1913, with the death of John O'Leary, even Yeats believed that 'Romantic Ireland's dead and gone'. After 1916, those perceptions were 'all changed, changed utterly'.

There was another element, the Labour movement, whose leaders, James Larkin and James Connolly, were militant syndicalist and revolutionary socialist respectively. They were determined to shake the exploitative power of capitalism, native and foreign, and establish decent working and living conditions for the inhabitants of some of the most overcrowded and least sanitary slums in Europe. They were victims of a mean and deep-seated social conservatism, common to much of the old establishment and some of the more well-to-do, pious elements of the new.

The European war came, and, for the first time in a century, Britain was embroiled. Home rule was put on ice, with everyone knowing that it was not the final word. John Redmond committed the Irish Volunteers to fight with the British empire for the rights of small nations without obtaining even before the rising any goodwill dividend. Just as the long-awaited moment of opportunity arrived, it encountered a strong British recruitment drive encouraged by the parliamentary nationalist leadership. There was a sinking feeling that, notwithstanding all the cultural effort of the previous twenty years, Ireland now faced an acute and imminent danger of being submerged in an overpowering imperial struggle and losing forever the threads of its separate national identity.

The 1916 rising was essentially a demonstration that Ireland was unsubdued, the latest in a long line of such actions. Nevertheless, the stakes were dramatically raised. The national demand expressed in the proclamation of the republic was for full sovereign independence, not home rule. Military action by a small breakaway minority repudiated the rules of British constitutionalism. Pearse summoned the ghosts of the past to stand with him, inspired by Cú Chulainn and what he called in his exalted frame of mind, the four 'gospels' of nationalism: Tone, Davis, Lalor and Mitchel. The rising was initially unpopular, and had no democratic mandate. That would come later.

The school at St Enda's occupied the Hermitage in Rathfarnham, the former home of Sarah Curran's father, evoking strong memories of Robert Emmet. The rising had a subsidiary purpose of vindicating the honour of Dublin after the muted role played by the city in 1798 and 1803, and re-establishing it as the capital of a free nation in place of its identification with the pale and castle rule.

The 1916 proclamation, though shorter, more eloquent and more vigorous, was modelled on Emmet's proclamation of 1803, which had been entitled 'The Provisional Government to the people of Ireland'. The earlier 1803 proclamation had declared that their object was 'to establish a free and independent republic in Ireland' and that it would commit as soon as possible its authority to an elected assembly of the people. The 1916 proclamation was in that respect along similar lines.

The 1916 proclamation bears the same relationship to our present-day republic as the American declaration of independence to the United States. In both cases, the achievement of an actual treaty-based independence, followed by international recognition, came six or seven years later, after a good deal of further fighting. Both documents are the founding charters of independent states. Both documents are a statement of justification for taking up arms against Britain, but also an appeal for public support on the basis of a manifesto. They had an immediate importance as a challenge to ruling authority, but also a long-term importance for the character of the state that was to follow.

The proclamation is addressed to Irishmen and Irish-women, all of whom, later on, are promised the suffrage, a position in advance of the Irish Parliamentary Party.

The appeal to the dead generations and the old tradition of nationhood was a bold claim to an all-embracing historical legitimacy. Read closely, the proclamation did not appeal exclusively to the physical force tradition. In every generation the Irish people had asserted their right to national freedom, and six times in 300 years by arms. Similarly, the rising was not just the work of the secret IRB, but also of other organisations like the Volunteers and the Irish Citizen Army.

While external support came from two sources, 'her exiled children in America' and 'gallant allies in Europe', Ireland was 'relying in the first on her own strength'. Irish-American support and its influence on the internal politics of the United States was a vital factor in the winning of Irish independence, together with President Wilson's trail-blazing support from 1917 of the principle of national self-determination, the foundation of the twentieth century international order. Without the German gun runs into Howth and Rathcoole, organised by Casement, Childers and others, the 1916 rising would not have been materially possible. Europe and America were to be the key to Ireland's future, but Casement, who spent eighteen months in the Kaiser's Germany at war, had few illusions by the time he left about any particular German gallantry. The notion was probably inspired by cultural collaboration with German scholars, such as Kuno Meyer, on the Gaelic revival.

There was one important distinction between America and Germany. One was about to become Britain's most important friend and ally. The other was about to become a strategic enemy. 1916 was the last time a mainstream Irish movement threatened Britain's 'selfish strategic interest', to use northern secretary, Peter Brooke's phrase of 1990, and invoked the help of an enemy at war with Britain. One of de Valera's most important insights enunciated in America in 1920 was that the key to success was to forswear any threat to Britain's strategic interests, even though he infuriated Irish-American leaders by so doing.

The proclamation declared Ireland's full sovereign independence, and denied any long-held rights of usurped possession.

It affirmed classical political rights, religious and civil liberty (an inversion of the well-known Orange phrase), equal rights and equal opportunity to all its citizens, an inclusive policy of 'pursuing the happiness and prosperity of the whole nation and of all its parts', then coming to the most famous phrase of all, 'cherishing all the children of the nation equally'. This included in the nation the politico-religious minority, and was a statement on which, as my father as an historian wrote, there was no easy road back. That having ceased to be an issue, at any rate in this jurisdiction, it has since been transformed into a more liberal social message relating to the non-acceptance of deprivation among children.

There was a firm promise to establish 'a permanent national government', meaning a system of government, 'representative of all the people of Ireland and elected by the suffrages of all her men and women'. The commitment of Pearse and the 1916 leaders to establish a national democracy has been completely underestimated in historical commentary. There are many texts that support this, for example, Pearse's observation on Tone and Davis in *The Spiritual Nation:* 'If we accept the definition of Irish Freedom as 'the Rights of Man in Ireland', we shall find it difficult to imagine an apostle of Irish freedom who is not a democrat'.

In an article in 1908 on the university question, he wrote 'democratic Ireland, the Ireland that toils, the Ireland that matters is with us'. His essay, *The Sovereign People*, a concept which is firmly enshrined in our constitution, in the preamble and article 6, goes on to discuss what the nation may decide to do with property rights, and the relationship of private property to public enterprise. He says:

> There is nothing divine or sacrosanct in any of these arrangements; they are matters of purely human concern, matters for discussion and adjustment between the members of a nation, matters to be decided upon finally by the nation as a whole and matters in which the nation as a whole can revise or reverse its decision whenever it seems good in the common interest to do so.

Pearse went on to argue that 'the people are the nation; the whole people, all its men and women', and, specifically, that possession of property conferred no special right to govern. He attacked the notion that survived long after him that the possession of what is called 'a stake in the country' conferred any special right to represent the people. He cautioned:

> And in order that the people may be able to choose as a legislature and as government men and women really and fully representative of themselves, they will keep the choice actually or virtually in the hands of the people; in other words ... they will, if wise, adopt the widest possible franchise. To restrict the franchise in any respect is to prepare the way for some future usurpation of the rights of the sovereign people.

Ironically and paradoxically, the 1916 proclamation is the starting point of the modern constitutional republican tradition that is the basis of the independent Irish state, even though the rising has been used subsequently to justify further resort, without prior mandate, to physical force – ignoring the existence and implications of a democratically elected Irish government.

The final paragraphs of the proclamation placed the cause of the 'Irish Republic' under the protection of the 'Most High God', making it clear that this was no case of French-style secular republicanism. It also pleaded for an honourable conduct of war, of a piece with the open but costly military nature of the rising.

The establishment of Dáil Éireann in 1919, the declaration of independence and the democratic programme were about forging in earnest a separate Irish-based constitutional tradition from the sweeping victory of Sinn Féin in the 1918 general election. Part of the election platform was an explicit reassertion of the principles of the 1916 proclamation. The rejection of parliamentarianism related only to continued participation in the British parliament as a means of attaining Irish self-government.

The 1919 declaration of independence was first and foremost the assertion of the right of the Irish people to be a free people and a repudiation of English rule maintained by military occupation against the will of the people.

The purposes of complete independence were declared to be the following:

> to promote the common weal, to re-establish justice, to provide for future defence, to ensure peace at home and good will with all nations; and to constitute a national policy based upon the people's will, with equal rights and equal opportunity for every citizen.

This was a reflection of the classic responsibilities of government with little hint of social revolution. The tone of the declaration was more militant and less inclusive than the proclamation. The phrase 'we demand the evacuation of our country by the English Garrison', given the past use of the phrase, was ambiguous as to whether it referred just to the crown forces, or whether it included the mainly protestant landowners and officials, who had hitherto largely supported the British connection. There was in fact a large-scale evacuation of both, leaving behind by the time of the 1926 census a much smaller religious minority. To be fair, there had been a steady decline in each census from 1861, as the terms of trade moved from privilege to more equality. Archbishop Walton Empey once summed up the position in the two sentences from a southern protestant perspective: 'Life was not always easy down here. To put it bluntly, most of our people found themselves on the losing side in a revolution'.

Those who chose or were able to stay transferred their allegiance to the new state, though for some time after remained semi-detached from it. A closer identification with the virtues of independent Ireland and its more recent success came later, as mutually inflicted historical and religious wounds healed gradually, without endorsement of the means that brought it about.

The support of the Labour movement was vital to the success of the revolution. Labour did not contest the 1918 general election, but was still a force to be reckoned with. The democratic programme was a commitment to tackle the acute economic and social deprivation in Ireland at that time. It asserted that the nation's sovereignty extended over all private property and wealth, 'which must be subordinated to the public right and welfare'. Service to the nation meant a right to an adequate share of the produce of the nation's labour.

There was a particular emphasis on the welfare of children, the right to food, clothing and shelter. The accent in education was on educating 'citizens of a free and Gaelic Ireland', a precursor of the overriding priority that would be given to learning Irish in the nation's schools.

There was a promise to abolish the poor law and substitute 'a sympathetic native scheme for the nation's aged and infirm', but no reference as yet to unemployment assistance. Safeguarding the health and physical and moral well-being of the people is also referred to, with protective moral legislation round the corner.

Two paragraphs followed on economic development, mainly the exploitation of national resources, but also the recreation and invigoration of industries, the promotion of trade, and in an echo from the famine, restrictions on the export of vital foodstuffs.

Interestingly, in the light of our present EU membership, the final paragraph refers to cooperation with the governments of other countries 'in delivering a standard of social and industrial legislation with a view to general and lasting improvements in the conditions under which the working-classes live and labour'.

It was to be some time before the aspirations of their democratic programme were put into effect during the first generation of independence, and they have been greatly developed since. Very little could be done, until the period of conflict was over, and the country began to be rebuilt.

Some decades later in October 1963, Seán Lemass as taoiseach commented that the democratic programme of the first dáil was not a programme in the real sense or even an adequate definition of the principles that should inspire one, 'but an avowal of an intention to make national freedom, when won, the beginning of a continuing campaign to undo

all the economic and social consequences of national subjection'.

Irish republicanism was to some a very contingent principle, which could, if necessary, be discarded, in the face of
adamant British opposition. To others, it became an absolute
core principle, which could never be abandoned. Liam Lynch,
republican military leader during the Civil War, stated that a
republic having been declared he would live 'under no other
law'. A republic was eventually delivered, not without further cost, by fully political and democratic means, to all intents and purposes in 1937, and formally in 1949. The republican mainstream, working through more than one party
and not just Fianna Fáil that incorporated it in its title, devoted themselves as a prerequisite to national unity, to building this state, which only a small rump repudiated, a state
which is to date the only republic we have.

Republicanism in the past thirty years has also come to
be associated with the more militant section of the nationalist community in Northern Ireland with the aim of a united
Ireland, until recently to be created by force, if necessary. In
the light of the pain inflicted on individual communities by
the violence of the last thirty years, it is clear that a broad,
generous and socially caring approach is needed in place of a
more confrontational, coercive and implicitly majoritarian
outlook.

The founding documents of 1916 and 1919 relate primarily to the development of this state, which has turned
out to be a remarkably stable and successful democracy. To

find a philosophy that could underpin a united Ireland in the context of today, it would also be necessary to go further back, to Young Ireland and to the United Irishmen, to tap the wellsprings of a more broadly inclusive constitutional republicanism.

4

James Connolly and the Worker's Republic

Brian Hanley

Were history what it ought to be, an accurate literary reflex of the times with which it professes to deal, (then) the pages of history would be almost entirely engrossed with a recital of the wrongs and struggles of the labouring people. But history in general treats the working-class as the manipulator of politics treats the working man: that is, with contempt when he remains passive, and with derision, hatred and misrepresentation whenever he dares to throw off the yoke of social servitude … (and) Irish history has ever been written by the master class, in the interests of the master class.[1]

So begins James Connolly's *Labour in Irish History*, arguably the founding document of Irish socialist republicanism. It advanced the belief that an independent Irish republic could only be achieved by uprooting capitalism, replacing it with a new economic order under which the Irish working-class would control the means of production, distribution and exchange. In other words, a worker's republic. While James Connolly was not the first Irish socialist, or the first socialist to write about Ireland, the idea of a worker's republic is synonymous with his life's work.[2] For it was Connolly's work that claimed a central place for the working-class in Irish history and that placed class struggle as central to his idea of a republic. Without an understanding of class struggle Connolly argued 'Irish history is but a welter of unrelated facts, a hopeless chaos of sporadic outbreaks, treacheries, intrigues and massacres.'[3] Armed with such an understanding however, Irish history is seen more clearly as a struggle between rich and poor, landlord and tenant, worker and capitalist. That Connolly was a marxist obviously differentiated his vision from those of his contemporaries: his worker's republic *was* a different republic from that envisaged by Connolly's allies in 1916. However sympathetic to social justice men like Pádraig Pearse, Thomas McDonagh and Tom Clarke were, they were not revolutionary socialists. Neither were Connolly's colleagues William O'Brien and Tom Johnson who would go on to dominate the Irish labour movement for decades after his death.[4] Even more different still were those who later claimed his legacy such as Éamon de Valera.[5]

While after 1916 much of nationalist Ireland embraced Connolly's martyrdom it ignored or recoiled from his marxism, and many have sought to underplay his commitment to socialist ideology, arguing that he was an Irish patriot first and foremost. In fact, Connolly's belief in the centrality of class was crucial to his conception of a republic. When Connolly described Karl Marx as the 'greatest of modern think-ers' he was not simply paying homage to a then fashionable ideologue.[6] Marxist ideas permeate Connolly's writings. These ideas were not simply inspired by academic interest. For Connolly there was no wealthy benefactor to fund his hours of research in the National Library or to provide a quiet country retreat where he could apply the finishing touches to his writings.

Connolly's ideas emerged from years of experience and in-volvement in working-class struggle. It is truly remarkable that his analysis of Irish history and society, the first 'history from below' of Ireland, was written by a man who left school at eleven, who scraped out a living for himself and his family as a carter, factory worker, cobbler, journalist and trade union organiser in Edinburgh, Dublin, Belfast and New York, often only barely managing to stave off abject poverty.[7] As Pro-fessor Joseph Lee has written of Connolly, 'nobody has over-come so many material obstacles to write so illuminatingly about Irish history. The quality of his insights obliges one to continue to wrestle with him … he asked big questions, which remain of enduring relevance.'[8]

What were the concepts that informed Connolly's ideal of the worker's republic? The first manifesto of his Irish Socialist Republican Party in 1896 gives a flavour of some *minimum* demands: the immediate nationalisation of the rail-ways, canals and banks; the introduction of graduated in-come tax, a minimum wage, and a forty-eight hour week; free child care, free education, public control of schools, universal suffrage and commitment to public ownership of the economy.[9] Connolly refused to accept that private ownership had any role to play in the economy. The wealth producing assets of the community should be held by the community itself, with production and distribution of goods to take place under direct control of the community. There was no role for private capitalism because

> the capitalist ... is a parasite on industry; as useless as any other parasite in the animal or vegetable world. The working-class is the victim of this parasite ... and it is the duty of the working class to use every means in its power to oust this parasite from the position which enables it to prey on labour.[10]

As a marxist, Connolly saw history as a long catalogue of class conflict in which capitalism had become triumphant by robbing the working-class of the fruits of their labour. Social inequality did not exist simply because some were wealthier than others, because of accidents of birth or good or bad fortune. Inequality was an essential part of the capitalist system, because the wealth of the capitalists was based on their exploitation of the working-class. Connolly was not ambiguous about the means the working-class would have to use to remove the ruling-class and to take control of this wealth:

> when the capitalist kills us so rapidly for the sake of a few pence ... it would be suicidal to expect them to hesitate to slaughter us wholesale when their very existence as parasites was at stake.[11]

If change were to come it would have to be revolutionary. Therefore, the working-class was ultimately justified in 'using the weapon of force to dislodge the usurping class'.[12]

But Connolly did not make this statement lightly, not least because he abhorred the waste of war and armed conflict; despite or perhaps because of the fact that he was a former soldier. He was never a militarist, but he saw no other way in which the system could be changed. Capitalism meant conquest, subjection, war; to overthrow it, violence was justified.[13]

Nor was his vision of society inspired by a mechanical socialism that saw the construction of a new society as a great experiment in social engineering. He was first and foremost inspired by his own experiences and those of his family, his friends and workmates. His writings on the conditions of those who lived and laboured in Dublin show a deep compassion and solidarity. On the question of women's rights, he asked 'of what use can be the establishment of any form of Irish state if it does not embody the emancipation of womanhood?' Such views were ahead of their time even for radicals of that era, and he described movingly how the female worker was the 'slave of a slave'.[14] Prophetically he warned those who made a fetish of state control that it alone was not enough to guarantee equality. To those that cried 'make this or that the property of the government' he answered 'yes, but only in proportion as the workers make government their property.' This conception of socialism, Connolly believed, would 'destroy at one blow all the fears of a bureaucratic state, ruling and ordering the lives of every individual from above.'[15] His socialism was based on the vision of a better society for the working-class, not simply a better organised one. Perhaps

Connolly's experience of rank and file industrial trade unionism in Ireland and the United States gave him a clearer
conception of working class democracy than other socialist
writers, who thought of the working-class purely in theoretical terms.

Because he saw class as the key division in Irish society,
Connolly was scathing about simplistic nationalist concep-
tions of Irish history. In *Labour in Irish History* he describes
the careers of various patriotic heroes of the past as efforts by
them to retain or regain lands and privilege in Ireland for
their own interests, not those of the Irish poor. The Jacobites
during the Williamite Wars had fought the English simply to
keep for themselves the 'lands of the native peasantry' not
because of love of Ireland. Daniel O'Connell, the 'Liberator'
had used and abused the peasant masses that followed him at
every turn. To those who defined their politics by their de-
votion to 'Ireland' Connolly explained:

> Ireland, without her people, is nothing to me, and the man
> who is bubbling over with love and enthusiasm for Ireland and
> can yet pass through our streets and witness all the wrong and
> suffering, shame and degradation without burning to end it is a
> fraud and a liar no matter how pleased he is to love the chemi-
> cal elements he calls Ireland.[16]

So liberty for Ireland could not simply mean political independence; it could not simply mean national unity against
the British. As he sarcastically wrote:

> Let us free Ireland says the patriot who won't touch socialism.
> Let us all join together and c-r-r-rush the br-r-rutal Saxon. Lets

us join together, says he, all classes and creeds. And says the town worker, after we have crushed the Saxon and freed Ireland what will we do? Oh then you can go back to your slums, same as before. And says the agricultural worker, after we have freed Ireland, what then? Oh, then you can go scraping around for the landlord's rent or the money-lender's interest, same as before. Whoop it up for liberty. After Ireland is free, says the Patriot who won't touch socialism, we will protect all classes, and if you won't pay your rent you will be evicted same as now. But the evicting party will wear green uniforms and the Harp without the Crown and the warrant turning you out on the roadside will be stamped with the arms of the Irish republic. Now isn't that worth fighting for?[17]

For Connolly it was impossible to believe that the 'class which is grinding us down can at the same time be leading us forward to national liberty.'[18] Connolly then was no nationalist.

But it would be wrong to infer from this, as many have done, that Connolly's participation in the 1916 rising was an aberration, an abandonment of his socialism in favour of nationalism; a negation of his life's work.[19] From an early stage in his career Connolly argued that it would be impossible to achieve socialism in an Ireland that was not independent:

the subjection of one nation to another, as of Ireland to the authority of the British Crown, is a barrier to the free political and economic development of the subjected nation, and can only serve the interests of the exploiting classes of both nations.[20]

In Ireland during the early twentieth century there was no escaping the issues of self-government, home rule or political independence and Connolly did not try to escape them. There could be no worker's republic within the framework of the British empire or the United Kingdom. Connolly did argue however, that the only people who could be trusted to carry through a fight for Irish independence were the people he claimed that had never betrayed Ireland: the working-class. While landlords, businessmen, farmers and middle-class intellectuals might claim to desire Irish freedom in the end they would always compromise; only the working-class was incorruptible. Furthermore in *Labour and Irish History* he sought to argue that native Gaelic society prior to the Anglo-Norman conquest had been egalitarian – that there had been a Gaelic principle of common ownership and that both feudalism and capitalism were therefore foreign importations.[21] Socialism was not achievable without independence, *but* neither was independence achievable without socialism. As Connolly famously argued:

> if you remove the English army tomorrow and hoist the green flag over Dublin Castle, unless you set about the organisation of the socialist republic your efforts would be in vain. England would still rule you. She would rule you through her capital-ists, through her landlords, through her financiers, through the whole array of commercial and individualist institutions she has planted in this country.[22]

In that sense, Connolly did not stray from the path of social-ism in 1916: he had always seen the struggle for the worker's republic as being intertwined with national independence.

It was the great failure of European socialism to oppose the First World War and the resulting slaughter in the trenches that convinced Connolly that he had no option but to throw in his lot with radical insurrectionist nationalism.[23] He did not do so from a position of strength. The defeat of the Dublin workers in 1913 had further narrowed his options. Ironically, the lockout had also seen a number of the radical nationalists, such as Pádraig Pearse and Tom Clarke, take a more sympathetic view of labour.[24] We can argue with some confidence that in the 1916 proclamation the commitment to universal male and female suffrage and to cherishing the children of the nation equally are due in large part to Connolly's influence, though these concepts fall far short of his wider vision.

After his death Connolly safely entered the pantheon of Irish nationalist heroes. His ideas were never simply forgotten or totally glossed over, as the fact that Connolly held radical views was too obvious to hide. However, more often than not in southern Irish society, he was presented as a republican with a pronounced social conscience or a dedicated labour activist but not the marxist revolutionary he was.

More nuanced critiques of Connolly's ideas emerged from the 1960s onwards. Scholars noted how Connolly had exaggerated the extent of common ownership in Celtic Ireland to back up his arguments in favour of notions of 'Celtic communism.'[25] His attacks on nationalist leaders such as Daniel O'Connell completely ignored O'Connell's progressive stance on issues such as slavery.[26] His desire to incorporate Wolfe Tone and Fintan Lalor into a socialist narrative ignored their own distinctive bourgeois radicalism. Connolly also did not see that a measure of national independence clearly was possible without revolutionary social change. Most importantly

Connolly, and he was far from unique in this, had failed to appreciate the depth of Ulster protestant opposition to self-government, let alone independence.

Connolly had worked as a union organiser in Belfast and realised that while in theory the highly industrialised, proletarian city should be ripe for socialist organisation, in reality there were bitter sectarian divisions among the working-class. He was convinced that Ulster unionism as an ideology only served 'the interests of … rack renting landlords and sweating capitalists.' Therefore, and despite its progressive potential, the north-east of Ulster had become 'the happy hunting ground of the slave driver and of the least rebellious slaves in the world.'[27] Yet, despite his belief that north and south would 'again clasp hands' as in 1798, and that 'the pressure of common exploitation' would make 'enthusiastic rebels' of the protestant working-class and 'earnest champions of religious and civil liberty' of their catholic counterparts, he failed to explain how the cause of the worker's republic could win support from northern protestant workers.[28] In theoretical and practical terms it was his greatest weakness.

Yet while often valuable, the critiques of Connolly have failed to explain the lasting attraction of his ideas. Throughout the twentieth century Irish radicals have returned to Connolly for inspiration or guidance. There is 'Connollyite' influence in the original democratic programme of the first dáil, before it was modified and moderated at the insistence of Michael Collins, among others.[29] Some of the factory and workplace occupiers of the revolutionary years (1919–23) raised the slogan of the worker's republic.[30] The anti-treaty IRA leader Liam Mellows in his 'Notes from Mountjoy' in 1922, argued that the idea of the worker's republic could have garnered wider backing for the anti-treatyite forces from workers unimpressed by the barren social programme of anti-treaty Sinn Féin.[31] During the treaty debates Countess Markievicz had claimed to owe her allegiance to the banner of the worker's republic.[32]

In the post civil war period radicals seized on Connolly's ideas to explain the victory of conservatism in the new free state. Peadar O'Donnell and George Gilmore, among others, argued that those with no interest in social change had been allowed to lead the struggle for independence, inevitably leading to betrayal and compromise. Only a struggle based on the working-class and their rural allies could have achieved a real republic. Throughout the late 1920s they attempted to convince the republican movement of this. The IRA's Saor Éire programme of 1931 with its promise to 'organise and consolidate the Republic of Ireland on the basis of the possession and administration of the workers and working farmers, the land and instruments of production and exchange' is clearly in the tradition of Connolly and the result of both O'Donnell and Gilmore's influence and the radicalising impact of the great depression on Ireland.[33] The founding statement of the Republican Congress in Athlone three years later in 1934, that declared 'we believe a republic of Ireland will never be achieved except through a struggle that uproots capitalism on its way' again restates the Connolly position. For a brief period the Congress drew support from as diverse an audience as miners in Castlecomer, building workers in Dublin, labourers in Achill, former IRA volunteers and Belfast protestant socialists. Ironically, that movement would suffer a split precisely over the question of whether or not to campaign openly for a worker's republic. In 1936 at the urging of former congress members Michael Price and Connolly's own son Roddy, the Irish Labour Party declared the worker's republic as its ultimate objective.[34]

The problem, of course, was that the idea of the worker's republic was always a minority one. The small groups of socialists and communists who identified with it failed to win an audience during the 1920s and 1930s, and the more influential republican organisations only tended to adopt it in periods of crisis and schism, such as in 1922 and 1934.[35] Mellows turned to the idea of the worker's republic only while in jail, having failed to raise the issue while he was at liberty.[36] Even when adopted from a seemingly strong position, the slogan drew accusations of communism: both the IRA in 1931 and the Labour Party in 1937 retreated in the face of intense clerical hostility to their leftward shift.[37] From the 1930s onwards the merest hint of radicalism was enough to draw the charge of communism – a charge very few in the labour or republican movement wished to face and which they invariably went out of their way to reject. The revival of Connolly's ideas inside the republican movement of the 1960s produced controversy with many refusing to recognise his marxism even then.[38]

James Connolly and the Worker's Republic

The idea of the worker's republic has always been a minority one within Irish republican thought, never gaining supremacy over the more conventional notions of republicanism. Yet its survival is due to the enduring relevance of class division, that great unmentionable concept for so many commentators on Irish history, and the fact that many of the major questions Connolly asked remain unanswered, even as our own republic congratulates itself on its prosperity.

5

The Unreal Republic

Fintan O'Toole

When he was asked during the Spanish Civil War to contribute to a set of statements on the conflict by writers, Samuel Beckett's reply was typically laconic. Beckett's answer came on a card on which was printed simply UPTHEREPUBLIC! As a declaration of support for the Spanish republic in its fight against the military uprising led by General Franco, this could hardly be more straightforward and unambiguous. But at a more private level, the message also carried something else that was typical of Beckett, a sardonic irony. For one of the great Irishmen of the twentieth century, it was easier to declare support for a Spanish republic than for an Irish republic. By taking possession of an Irish slogan that had been used by both Sinn Féin and Fianna Fáil, and that had little appeal for him, Beckett was making a joke on both himself and Ireland. He knew very well that in Ireland being a republican meant something quite different from what it meant in a broader European context. Beckett thus summarised in thirteen letters the strange situation of a country in which people who regarded themselves as republican might be at odds with the political realities of the republic itself.

The notion of republican democracy has deep roots in Irish political history and after 1916 it became the framework within which the Irish state emerged. The Irish republic existed both as a goal that would be realised some day when Ireland was united and as an emerging reality in the state that took shape between the early 1920s and the late 1940s. For well over half a century now, it has been normal for most people living in the twenty-six counties to say that they come from 'The Republic'. Yet it is not entirely accidental that even the use of this word to describe the state is mired in confusion and ambivalence. The constitution declares the name of the state to be Ireland or Éire. The Republic of Ireland Act of 1948 declares that 'the description of the state shall be the Republic of Ireland', but the constitution has never been amended along these lines. In bringing forward the Republic of Ireland Bill in 1948, the then taoiseach John A. Costello, explained that there would be a difference between what the state was called and what it was: 'There is the name of the state and there is the description of the state. The name of the state is Ireland and the description of the state is the Republic of Ireland.'[1] But even as a description, the republic barely exists. The official government website nowhere refers to the Republic of Ireland or even states that Ireland is a republic. In the diplomatic sphere, while the Irish state has accepted credentials from ambassadors addressed to 'Ireland', the 'Republic of Ireland', or the name of the president, it will not accept credentials addressed to the 'Irish Republic' because this last term was the name used in the declaration of independence in 1919 and encompassed all thirty-two counties.

All of this has, of course, little effect on the view most of the state's citizens take of their country, but the confusion is, in its own way, rather apt. If we're not sure whether to call our state a republic or not, it's partly because it is and it isn't. In the sense in which most people use the word – a liberal democracy without a monarch – Ireland obviously is a republic. But a broader notion of republicanism raises basic questions about the reality of Ireland's democracy. Using the definition articulated so powerfully in the work of Philip Pettit, we can ask whether Ireland is:[2]

> a state that can operate effectively against private domination, helping to reduce the degree of domination people suffer at the hands of other individuals and groups ... a state that is organised in such a way that it will not itself represent a source of domination in people's lives ... a state that is conducted for the public interest, that pursues its policies in the public eye, and that acts under public control – a state that is truly a *res publica*, a matter of public business?

The short answer to those questions is 'not really'.

The creation of a republic in Pettit's deeper sense isn't a matter of reading a declaration outside the GPO or even of enacting a constitution. It is a process that unfolds over time and that has to be renewed constantly, creatively, and with passion. In the Irish case, that process has been hampered by a number of powerful forces. All of them are reasonably obvious but because they come from different directions, their cumulative effect has been hard to define. What they have in common is the way they have imposed limits on the emergence of a republican democracy in which public business is conducted openly, fairly, and for the public interest.

One set of limits derived from the overwhelmingly catholic nature of the state established after partition. The catholic church didn't just enjoy the spiritual allegiance of a large majority of the population. It was also a major temporal power, with direct control over large elements of what would be regarded as the public realm in other democracies. The health and education systems were church-dominated. Specifically catholic teaching was embodied in law in a number of areas, mostly those that related to sexuality, reproduction and marriage. So, while the state was far from the simple theocracy of caricature, it was unquestionably subject to a huge degree of direct and indirect church influence. Practically all politicians accepted this influence as right and proper. In presenting his new constitution in 1937, Éamon de Valera proclaimed bluntly that it would present Ireland to the world 'as a Catholic nation'. This attitude was echoed, and even enhanced by the other political parties. When it took office in 1948, the Inter-Party coalition government immediately sent a message of homage to Pope Pius XII expressing its:

> desire to repose at the feet of Your Holiness the assurance of our filial loyalty and our devotion to your August Person, as

well as our firm resolve to be guided in all our work by the teachings of Christ and to strive for the attainment of a social order in Ireland based on Christian principles.[3]

The effects of this subordination of state policy to church teaching on the kind of individual freedoms that citizens might expect in a republic were obvious. It is also worth noting, however, that these notions of 'filial loyalty', in which the church was the stern but loving father and the state the faithful and obedient son, gave free rein to an aristocratic imagery that was, on the face of it, at odds with republican notions of civic and political equality. Having shrugged off one culture of deference to titled nobles, the new state embraced another. The elected representatives of the people always kneeled before a bishop and kissed his ring. The fact that the bishop was addressed as 'My Lord' and lived in a house that was always called a palace, did not seem to cause any great discomfort to Irish people who would have been enraged by any suggestion that Ireland should honour an aristocracy.

That deference is well and truly gone, and the political power of the church collapsed with remarkable rapidity in the 1990s. But it has left behind a problematic legacy. The real problem with church dominance of public services in a democracy is that the church itself is, explicitly and emphatically, not a democracy. It is a hierarchical organisation in which decisions come from the top down. Ideas of openness, transparency and accountability are largely irrelevant to the way it operates. And while that may not be a problem for citizens in their spiritual lives, it becomes a very severe problem indeed when key parts of the state, especially in its health and education systems, are effectively controlled by the church. The most extreme manifestation of this problem in recent years has been the way church authorities dealt with revelations of child abuse by priests, brothers and nuns by seeing these basic issues of human rights and legality as essentially internal matters governed by canon law and the short-term interests of the institution. But there is also a less dramatic, but no less corrosive, conflict between, on the one hand, republican notions of the equal entitlement of citizens to public goods, and, on the other, the persistence of private church power in the provision of those goods. It is by no means an irresolvable conflict but it is one that needs to be recognised in an increasingly diverse and multicultural society.

The second obvious set of limitations on the emergence of a republic in Ireland has been the way the very notion of republicanism, which ought to act as a bulwark against private domination, has instead been an instrument of private domination. The language of Irish political discourse, in which a republican means someone who is associated with or supports the IRA expresses this paradox. The existence throughout the history of the state of a secret and self-appointed cabal, accountable to no one but itself but claiming to act on behalf of the Irish republic, has tended to discredit the idea of republicanism. It has brought a mixture of tragedy and farce to any discussion of the subject. When a secret body claims to be 'the Government of Ireland', as the IRA army council has done, the whole notion of popular sovereignty is thrown into comic absurdity. When it then goes on to claim the right to use extreme violence on behalf of the people, that notion is foulled with blood and madness.

Less directly, the ideology of this kind of republicanism has had a broader effect on political life in the twenty-six counties. It interacted with mainstream political national-ism to create the feeling that the Irish state was a temporary arrangement, at best a mere way-station on the road to the true republic of a United Ireland that would emerge at some time in the future. In the 1980s, the former taoiseach Charles Haughey remarked that 'When I talk about my Ireland I am talking about something that is not yet a complete reality. It is a dream that has not yet been fulfilled.' This feeling that the state was unreal, dream-like and incomplete was rooted in the political rhetoric that defined the republic as the en-tity declared in 1916 and that had never been created. The ambivalence of much of the political class about the state it governed added to the feeling that a real republic was, in a sense, an impossible concept, relegated to the realm of aspi-rations, and therefore beyond the reach of practical politics.

The third limitation on the process of creating an Irish republic is corruption. If, in Pettit's phrase, a republic is a 'state that is conducted for the public interest', then corrup-tion is the antithesis of republicanism. Political corruption is the subordination of the public interest to private interest. Its purpose is mirrored in its means of operation: it is carried out beyond public scrutiny, as a set of private understand-ings. But it also requires a corrosion of the idea of the public interest itself. Political decisions that are made for private reasons – to favour those who have favoured the politician – have to be justified by reference to an invented set of public policies. This is a wider process, and one that has in some cases drawn the institutions of the state – including the oireachtas, the justice system, the revenue commissioners and the civil service – into unknowing collusion with corruption.

It is generally held at the moment that the disillusionment with democracy that is evident in the low turnouts in recent elections has been caused by the revelations of the various tribunals of inquiry that have become a semi-permanent feature of Irish public life. But it is worth remembering that long before the Irish political landscape was dominated by tribunals of inquiry into the corrupt practices of the 1980s and 1990s, Irish people understood quite well that they lived in a democracy where influence and power could be bought. The idea of 'pull', where jobs, grants and state services were assumed to be subject to the rule that 'It's not what you know but who you know' was pervasive in Irish life. Most people probably saw the doings of their political masters as simply a larger version of this general rule.

It's worth looking back on an MRBI poll conducted for an RTE *Today Tonight* programme in November 1991. To the proposition that: 'there is a Golden Circle of people in Ireland who are using power to make money for themselves', a massive eighty-nine per cent agreed. Eighty-one per cent agreed that the people in this golden circle were made up in equal measure of business people and politicians. Seventy-six per cent thought the scandals that were then beginning to emerge were 'part and parcel' of the Irish economic system rather than one-off events. Eighty-three per cent thought that the then current scandals were merely 'the tip of the iceberg', while eighty-four per cent said business people involved in corrupt dealings and fraud got off more lightly than other criminals.

These assumptions predate the tribunals and they remind us how little Irish people actually believed themselves to be living in a republic where the public interest was protected and all citizens interacted with the state as equals. Corruption, in this sense, was not a cloak-and-dagger affair, but a vivid pattern in the fabric of public life. Much of the political and business elite involved in the Ansbacher tax evasion scheme were shaping the world that Irish people live in, not just metaphorically but literally. Meanwhile, the abuse of non-resident accounts was an open secret throughout the banking industry in the 1980s and 1990s. The banking industry facilitated people who were known to be residents in claiming that they were non-residents so as to avoid paying DIRT. The 1999 report of the dáil committee of public accounts into the scandal found that there was a particularly close and inappropriate relationship between banking and the state and its agencies. 'The evidence suggests that the state and its agencies were perhaps too mindful of the concerns of the banks and too attentive to their pleas and lobbying', the report says.

The mixture of political corruption and conservative ideology that created and sustained this culture of tax evasion had huge long-term effects. It encouraged large sections of the Irish business class to salt away its disposable capital in unproductive offshore or bogus non-resident accounts rather than to invest it productively. It contributed to a fiscal crisis in which there was no option but to slash state spending on social programmes. This in turn meant that those who needed help were left to fend for themselves while those who had money were able to improve their relative position in society. While ordinary working people were paying tax at up to sixty per cent, many people with considerable resources were able to avail of amnesties at a rate of fifteen per cent or to evade tax altogether. When the boom came, the rich were in an even better position to benefit from it.

What became ever more apparent as the years went on and the revelations from the tribunals continued to unfold was that the ideal of the republic hadn't just slipped away in a process of economic and social change or been stolen from us by perfidious Albion. It had been deliberately and cynically betrayed from within. Some people at the very top of the heap had owed more loyalty to the Cayman Islands than to Ireland. Some citizens blessed with resources had turned themselves into 'bogus non-residents', here but not here, part of Ireland when the goodies were being given out but mysteriously vanishing into a virtual exile when the obligations of citizenship were to be met. And while everyone was equal before the law some people had turned out to be more equal than others.

The last set of limits to the emergence of a republic has been the growth of the notion that the state is an entity in itself, with interests of its own that are not necessarily the same as the public interest. This is not the kind of thing that gets stated explicitly, but it has hovered around some of the political controversies of the last fifteen years. It popped up in the Tribunal of Inquiry into the Beef Processing Industry in 1991 when the then attorney general stated that his role at the inquiry was not to represent the public interest but the state. It arose in the traumatic controversy over the infection of hundreds of women with hepatitis C by a state agency, the Blood Transfusion Service, when the state ended up fighting a dying woman, Brigid McCole, in court as if the state and a wronged citizen were somehow natural enemies. It ran through a series of court cases in the 1990s in which the parents of disabled children tried to get an appropriate education for their children. In those cases, the state sought to establish once and for all that citizens have only such rights as the state is willing to grant them. This notion is based on the profound belief that the state is an entity up there above and beyond the people, with a life and a will all of its own.

The last fifteen years or so has been a period in which some of these underlying limitations on the emergence of an Irish republic have been rolled back, while other problems have emerged. On the positive side of the equation, the shrinking of the political power of the catholic church to the kind of scale it ought to have in a democratic republic has opened up the possibility of a pluralist culture in which the idea of shared civic values is at least up for discussion. The Northern Ireland peace process and the gradual dismantling of paramilitarism has created the opportunity for the idea of republicanism to be taken back from the gunmen. The tribunals and inquiries, problematic as they are, have at least shone a retrospective light onto the nature of the relationship between business and politics. Some basic safeguards in the form of ethics legislation and limits of political donations have been put in place. The Freedom of Information Act has improved the climate of transparency in which the state and public bodies operate. The growing influence of European legislation has, in many cases, had a reasonable effect on governance, making, for example, tendering for public projects more open.

All of these processes are incomplete, however. The groundswell of change that gathered in the early 1990s has either stalled or receded. Democratic control over the health and education systems is barely being discussed. The peace process lost momentum and became mired in ambivalence. The revelations about corruption and tax evasion have lost their impact through weariness, cynicism, and the fact that few of those who have been exposed have suffered any great penalty. The Freedom of Information Act has been weakened.

At the same time, there are new challenges. The republican ideal is one that has been associated with the nation state, and in the Irish context it has to be made real in the context of a society that is, according to the international

Globalisation Index, the most globalised in the world. The growing cult of money, celebrity and beauty means that certain people no longer have to do anything at all in order to generate massive media coverage which in turn confers on them a new kind of twenty-first century aristocracy. The emergence of a multi-cultural Ireland has also changed the context. On the one hand, it could give a huge boost to the idea of an Irish republic by highlighting the need for a concept of citizenship that is available to all regardless of creed or ethnic origin. On the other, if it is mishandled, it could lead to the emergence of a reactionary attempt to define citizenship in precisely those terms or to create a hierarchy of belonging in which some citizens are more Irish than others.

Most crucially of all, the limits of republicanism itself present us with a challenge. The great weakness of republican thinking has always been its struggle to connect a notion of political equality in which each citizen has the same weight in the determination of the public good, with the reality of economic inequality in which some citizens obviously carry more weight than others. The Ireland that has been emerging over the last decade is one in which there has been greater prosperity but also an ever-widening gap between rich and poor. This imbalance of power cannot be disconnected from the public realm. Not only do state policies and actions have a profound effect on who wins and who loses in the competition for resources, but we also get the irony that those who depend most on the state – children, the poor, the disabled, the sick, the old – also have least say in setting the

state's agenda. They may have the same right to vote as everyone else, but political power is determined by far more than
votes. Access to the media, the ability to campaign, the ability
to exert economic pressure, the power to threaten dire consequences – all of these can determine the actions of the state
just as much as the votes of the electorate do. Republican
democracy has to be given a content that goes beyond the
nature of political institutions and that content has to centre
on equality.

For all these challenges, however, the republic is still an
ideal that can frame the search for a public morality in the
new Ireland. It still contains many of the things that people
at the start of the twentieth century, about to embark on the
painful process of inventing a modern nation, wanted from
it: a sense of justice, a feeling of belonging, a capacity to be
proud of ourselves, a notion, however vague, that there was
an 'ourselves' to be proud of.

The precise content of that notion was hard to pin down
then, but it was made concrete and tangible by its obvious
absence. In an odd way, all of the revelations of the last decade, by pointing up the absence of a public community of
which Irish people could be proud, served to remind them
that they still wanted one. The joys of shopping, however
enthusiastically embraced, didn't quite fill the hole where a
society called 'Ireland' should be. Retail therapy didn't quite
assuage the anguish of finding ourselves at the start of a new
century, right back where we had started the old one, in an un-
settled, fluid place that needed to be re-invented as a republic.

6

Law in a Republic

Ivana Bacik

Is Ireland a republic? This might seem like a simple question – but one to which there is no simple answer.

First, the word 'republic' has many meanings. So in trying to answer this question the language of republicanism must be examined. This is always complex, and nowhere more so than here in Ireland.

Republicanism is generally understood as the political theory supporting a system where the government is elected by the people for a limited term, rather than consisting of a dictator or hereditary monarch in office for life. The word derives from the Latin *res publica* or 'public affair', suggesting that control of governance lies with the people – the citizens. A republic is a state based upon concepts of popular sovereignty, of democracy, and of the protection of basic liberties of the citizen.

Of course, at a wider level the conception of popular

sovereignty is under increasing threat. It may be argued that in every nation state, popular sovereignty is being undermined by the growing power of corporations – and by a worldwide neo-liberal economic system that turns citizens into consumers. In post-celtic tiger Ireland, this danger is clear, and we would do well to guard against undue encroachments on our popular sovereignty from multinational corporate interests, unaccountable to any public. In a less sinister way, the sovereignty of individual nation states is also being affected by the growing power of regional transnational organisations like the European Union. That is why it is so important that the EU and other groupings of states should develop strong mechanisms for ensuring democratic accountability, for structures enabling the people to have a say in how they are run.

The idea of popular sovereignty is closely associated with another distinguishing feature of republics – the need for checks and balances against the abuse of power. The people delegate the power to govern to their elected representatives, and are protected against abuse of power by these representatives through the doctrine of separation of powers. This doctrine requires that legislative, executive and judicial powers are exercised by three separate arms of government. Thus the legislature or parliament has the exclusive power to make laws. The executive or government has power only to implement those laws; and the power of the judiciary is limited to adjudicating on the application and interpretation of those laws.

The Republic

Harking back to the French revolution, republicans are anti-monarchy and anti-clerical, believing in the need for a complete separation of church and of state, so that the will of the citizens as a whole may prevail, irrespective of their individual religious affiliations. For French republicans like Rousseau, the sovereign legislature thus consisted of the whole people, and the community incorporated every member as an indivisible part of the whole.

Contemporary theories of republicanism focus upon the idea of a system of governance that selects all that is best in divided or factional interests and distils them in the name of the public interest or 'common good'. Of course the balance between individual liberties and the common good is a complex one, and different approaches are taken by those identifying themselves as liberals; as opposed to communitarians; or in John Rawls' terms, as civic humanists. Liberal republicans tend to emphasise individual freedoms at the expense of the common good, and to believe in the need to separate public and private spheres. Republicans at the communitarian end of the political spectrum conversely emphasise the need to achieve a common good, sometimes at the expense of individual freedoms, and see the private and public spheres as intertwined.

Of course, in this very abstract debate, one woman's republicanism may well be another's liberalism, and terms are bandied about wildly with all sorts of different meanings ascribed to them.

Clearly, the word republicanism can have many diverse

meanings. Here in Ireland, it has been especially problematic. Historically, we speak of the men and women of the
1916 rising as being republicans, since they sought independence through the overthrow, rather than the gradual end, of
British rule. Fianna Fáil, as we know, refers to itself – or at
least used to refer to itself – as 'the Republican Party'. Nowadays, the term republican is more likely to refer to supporters
of Sinn Féin or the IRA; that is, to those who support or supported violence as a means of establishing a republic encom-
passing the whole island of Ireland.

Thus the language of republicanism in Ireland is particularly complex, because it has come to be synonymous with
support of one specific political party closely associated with
a paramilitary organisation. So while we may proudly describe ourselves as living in a republic, many of us would hesitate to call ourselves 'republicans'.

Of course this is not an unique Irish difficulty. In the US,
to describe oneself as 'republican' also carries very particular
meaning, implying support for George W. Bush's warmon-
gering Republican Party – and opposition to the Democratic
Party. It thus conveys a great deal of ideological baggage –
from a hatred of Michael Moore to a tendency to call chips
'freedom fries'.

Linguistic difficulties do not stop at the word 'republican'. Even the use of the word 'republic' in an Irish context
requires clarification. Contrary to popular view, the name of
this state is not 'the Republic of Ireland', nor could it be. Nowhere in the text of our constitution, Bunreacht na hÉire-

ann, is the word 'republic' used – because in 1937, when the constitution was adopted, Ireland was not a republic.

The Irish free state was still legally in existence then, but taoiseach Éamon de Valera, the architect of the 1937 constitution, appears to have deliberately omitted any reference to the actual status of the state, or to the word 'republic' within the text of the document. Yet in July 1945, in what became known as the 'Dictionary Republic' speech, he argued in the dáil that the free state was a republic in everything but name. Claiming that this was obvious on the facts, he observed trenchantly:

> The State is what it is, not what I say or think it is. How a particular State is to be classified politically is a matter not to be settled by the ipse dixit of any person but by observation of the State's institutions and an examination of its fundamental laws … look up any standard book of reference and get … any definition of a republic or any description of what a republic is and judge whether our State does not possess every characteristic mark by which a republic can be distinguished or recognised. We are a democracy with the ultimate sovereign power resting with the people – a representative democracy with the various organs of State functioning under a written Constitution, with the executive authority controlled by Parliament, with an independent judiciary functioning under the Constitution and the law, and with a Head of State directly elected by the people for a definite term of office.[1]

Thus the new constitution created what was to all intents and purposes a republic – although not one based upon the secular principles of French republicanism, given the theocratic influences obvious in the language of the preamble and fundamental rights articles, as we shall see.

De Valera's flexible approach to definitional difficulties might well deserve the description 'an Irish solution to an Irish problem.' But his verbal acrobatics have had a long-lasting legacy. Article 4 of the Irish constitution still declares, simply: 'The name of the State is Éire, or in the English language, Ireland.'

Even after the constitution was adopted, for some years the Irish state continued its membership of the British Commonwealth. It was only in 1948 that the Republic of Ireland Act was passed, section 2 of which states: 'It is hereby declared that the description of the State shall be the Republic of Ireland'. Ironically, it was not Fianna Fáil – the republican party – which introduced this act, but a government led by taoiseach John A. Costello of Fine Gael.

The new taoiseach announced his intention to declare the state a republic at a press conference in Canada on 7 September 1948, having won an election that after sixteen years finally saw Fianna Fáil out of office. The Republic of Ireland Act was formally inaugurated on 18 April (Easter Monday) 1949 and was presented as an almost technical legislative measure. As the taoiseach said during the second stage of the bill:

> [It] ... will put beyond all doubt dispute and controversy our international status and our constitutional position. It will also, we hope and sincerely believe, end all that crescendo of bitterness which has been poisoning our country for the past 25 or 26 years, and it will also enable us to do that which, from the discussions which have already taken place in Dáil Éireann on the Bill, is the earnest hope of all Parties in this Parliament,

improve our relations not merely with Canada, Australia, New Zealand and South Africa, but particularly with our nearest neighbour and best customer, Great Britain.[2]

Fond hopes indeed!

So in other words, the basis for the status of the Irish republic is statutory and not constitutional. Notably, this 'description' of the state as a republic does not change the name of the state, which as we know from article 4 of the constitution is simply 'Ireland'. Thus, since 1937 and even since 1948, the official name for the state is just that – 'Ireland'.

This difference between the name of the state, and its description, has led to various legal difficulties. In 1989, for example, in the *Ellis* case, Judge Walsh condemned the UK courts for referring in extradition warrants to 'the Republic of Ireland'.[3] He said that if foreign courts issue warrants in English, they must refer to the state according to its name in English – that is, 'Ireland' – in accordance with article 4. Further, he ruled that warrants which did not comply with this requirement should be returned to Britain for rectification by the courts there.

This persisting distinction between the name and description of our state is confusing and unwieldy. This may be one reason why the expert constitution review group recommended in 1996 that, to simplify matters, the English language text of article 4 should be amended to read 'The name of the State is Ireland' with the Irish language text to declare 'Éire is ainm don Stát'.[4] This obvious step has not yet been taken, and in any case would still not confer constitutional status upon the description of Ireland as a republic. Thus, we still have difficulty with Ireland as a republic in law.

But is de Valera right? Are we a republic in reality – a *de facto* republic, whatever the legal name or description of the state? The general view is that we are. But I think our status as a republic is contestable for at least two reasons. First, arguably, we have failed adequately to implement the separation of powers doctrine; and secondly, we have not fully separated church and state within our legal and political systems.

Before examining these two flaws in the republican status of Ireland, it is important to note that in one respect at least the Irish state conforms to a key precept of republican theory. The concept of popular sovereignty is clearly outlined in the constitution, the preamble of which provides: 'We, the people of Éire … Do hereby adopt, enact and give to ourselves this Constitution.' Further, article 6 states that 'All powers of government, legislative, executive and judicial, derive, under God, from the people … according to the requirements of the common good.'

This is a classic statement of republican theory, and the sovereignty of the Irish people is demonstrated in many practical ways – for example, by the election of TDs to Dáil Éireann; and by the use of the popular referendum as the only means to change the constitution itself, under article 46.

In a third important example of the effect of popular sovereignty, individuals may sue the Irish state for injuries caused by employees or agents of the state. In 1972, the supreme court held, in the landmark case of *Byrne v. Ireland*,

that the sovereign immunity granted to the British crown
against civil suit by its subjects had not survived the passing
of the 1937 constitution.[5] Thus the Irish state may be held
liable for injuries suffered by citizens, for which it is respon-
sible. The plaintiff was a woman who had been injured upon
falling into a hole dug by employees of the then department
of posts and telegraphs. According to this important decision, she was entitled to sue the state for damages sustained
as a result. Judge Walsh pointed out that:

> Under our own constitutional provisions it is the Oireachtas
> which makes the laws and it is the judiciary which administers
> them; there is no apparent reason why the activities of either
> of these organs of state should compel the State itself to be
> above the law.

Thus, we may reflect now that the origins of what is often
known as the 'compo culture' – where so many individuals take
personal injury actions against local authorities – lie in the
definition of popular sovereignty and the idea of a republic.

This development in the liability of the state is one feature of republicanism in practice. But the two flaws mentioned earlier remain, and will be dealt with in turn.

First, whatever Judge Walsh may have said, we lack the
basic commitment to the separation of powers doctrine that
is essential to the functioning of any real republic. There are
obvious reasons why the doctrine is so important. In particular, only the legislature should have the power to make
law. Members of the oireachtas, unlike judges, are elected
and accountable. It is they who should hold the government

to task over its failures. One danger with breaching this principle and allowing judges to make law is that judicial sub-
jectivism or personal bias can become enshrined as law.
When the majority of our judges are drawn from a middle
class background, then no matter how fair-minded they are
as individuals, their judgments may reflect a particular view
of society. Decisions on the constitutional freedom of association, for instance, have invariably been decided in favour of
employers, or individual employees, against trade unions –
attempts to use the provision to further collective rights
have generally failed. Similarly, our judges have been very
reluctant to use the constitutional equality guarantee to stop
discriminatory practices.

In fact, there has been a real breakdown of separation of
powers in our system. Although the principle is enshrined in
article 15 of our constitution, which states that: 'The sole
and exclusive power of making laws for the state is hereby
vested in the Oireachtas', the problem is that Irish legislators
have been most inactive in many areas, thrusting a lawmaking role upon judges. The courts have had to step into the
breach, in the context of government and legislative failures
to enact law on abortion; to provide an adequate immigration policy; to protect the rights of asylum-seekers or Irish-
born children; or to meet the needs of children with special
needs or children at risk.

It could even be argued that in some cases judges have
asserted popular sovereignty where both legislature and executive have notably failed. The decision in the *Crotty* case,

for example, established the need to hold a referendum on entry into international obligations impacting on national sovereignty.[6] But this is arguably not an appropriate role for judges to play, except as a last resort. Judges in a country with a written constitution must have a strong protective role against legislative abuse of power, and against breaches of citizens' rights – but to require them to step in just because of legislative inertia is another matter.

Judicial lawmaking of this kind can lead to uneasy and unsatisfactory compromise on policy matters, with a strong element of uncertainty, and tension, between the legislative and judicial functions. This sort of compromise does not ultimately make for good or effective policies in difficult areas, where democratic debate, conducted through the legislature, is really needed in order to achieve a more adequate resolution. Nor does it make for a properly functioning republic in the classic meaning of the term.

The other unique flaw in Ireland's status as a republic is that, far from being secular in the French tradition, our state has a distinctly theocratic aspect. This is partly due to the historical development of our legal system. Our common law system is based upon the English model, but prior to the Anglo-Norman invasion of 1170, a sophisticated indigenous system of law known as Brehon law prevailed throughout the land. This was associated with a system of tribal kings or provincial chiefs, and an important place was reserved for the early christian church. Triad 200 sums up Brehon governance as comprising: 'the three rocks to which lawful behaviour is tied: monastery, lord, kin.'[7]

The powerful place of the early christian church in Brehon law is mirrored by the powerful place of the catholic church in the emergence of the modern Irish republic. The church has wielded considerable power for a long time in Ireland. Particularly in the late eighteenth century, the drastic restrictions imposed upon the rights of catholics by the British state merely strengthened the church's position in society, and the will of the people to practise their chosen faith. Catholicism thus became the religion of social and political defiance, of nationhood and patriotic identity – a heady cocktail indeed.

Once catholic emancipation was formally secured, the church amassed significant power, gaining ownership and control of many schools, hospitals and social services across Ireland. After independence, it moved into alignment with those in power in the new free state, making its influence felt in every sphere of public life. As academic Maura Adshead has written, 'The Irish State, from the beginning, was ostentatiously catholic.'[8]

Even now, the church continues to act as a sort of 'shadow welfare state', supplanting the state's role in many ways. It also continues to hold vast tracts of valuable land. It wields great social and political power, despite the scandals over the sexual and physical abuse of children in the care and control of catholic religious orders, and despite grave public concern over the way in which the church attempted for so long to protect abusers within its ranks.

It is no coincidence that the president, members of the council of state and judges are required to take an oath beginning 'In the presence of Almighty God ...' and that the national broadcaster still carries a denominational religious message, the 'Angelus', at 6 p.m. every evening. No wonder that when we speak of 'Church and State', 'Church' always comes first.

The power of the church reached its peak during Éamon de Valera's first term as taoiseach in the 1930s, when he infamously consulted the catholic archbishop John Charles McQuaid for help in drafting the 1937 constitution. The archbishop's input into the wording of the fundamental rights articles 40 to 44 is especially notable. These articles guarantee a range of rights, such as rights to life and liberty, to equality, to one's good name, to freedom of expression and association; rights of the family, private property and freedom of religious practice. The article guaranteeing religious freedom originally referred to the 'special position' of the catholic church as 'the guardian of the Faith professed by the great majority of the citizens'. Although this provision was removed in 1972 by referendum, the strong influence of catholic doctrine is still evident elsewhere in the text of the constitution, the preamble of which begins 'in the name of the Most Holy Trinity ...' and article 6 of which provides that 'All powers of government, legislative, executive and judicial, derive, under God, from the people.'

However, theocratic ideology is most conspicuous in the language of the fundamental rights articles. Article 41.2 is perhaps the strongest reflection of this, providing that 'by her life within the home, woman gives to the State a support without which the common good cannot be achieved'. The same article commits the state to 'endeavour to ensure that mothers shall not be obliged by economic necessity to engage in labour to the neglect of their duties in the home.'

Theocracy is also alive and well in article 41, which guarantees the rights of the family 'the natural primary and fundamental unit group of society.' This article has been interpreted to preserve a particularly conservative definition of 'family', limited to that based upon marriage – in 1980 for example the supreme court held that an unmarried mother and her child did not constitute a family in the sense of article 41.

When they were first introduced, these articles were a novelty, at odds with the English concept of parliamentary supremacy with which the Irish judiciary had been trained. It took about twenty years for judges to become used to applying fundamental rights guarantees – in many cases with very broad subjective interpretations, often leading to breaches of the doctrine of separation of powers referred to earlier.

The watershed year came in 1963, when the supreme court heard the case of *Ryan v. Attorney General.*[9] The plaintiff had challenged legislation establishing a water fluoridation programme. Although she ultimately lost the case, the court held that a challenge like this could be based upon the right to bodily integrity – a right they said was implicit in article 40, which refers generally to 'the personal rights of the citizen.' The court ruled, invoking a papal encyclical, that this article implicitly guarantees a range of other – unwritten – rights, deriving from the 'Christian and democratic nature of the State'.

This decision marked the start of a period of extensive development of the 'natural law' doctrine of interpretation, whereby the courts implied into the constitution various rights, such as the right to earn a livelihood and the right to marital privacy.[10] This certainly meant that life was breathed into the previously under-used fundamental rights articles, but this activism had a shaky foundation. At times it appeared as if judges were simply drawing rights out of the air, from their own subjective moral or religious beliefs. The source of natural rights for some judges was expressly theological, derived from christian or more particularly catholic teaching.

This was really a very dangerous development, allowing a theocratic ideology to influence the emerging constitutional rights jurisprudence. It also allowed the personal prejudices of individual judges to be reflected in their legal decisions. In one notorious example, Chief Justice O'Higgins in the 1984 *Norris* case described homosexuality as 'unnatural sexual conduct which Christian teaching held to be gravely sinful'.[11]

Fortunately, the practice of invoking natural rights was finally expressed as falling out of judicial favour in 1995. That year the supreme court upheld the constitutionality of legislation regulating the provision of information on abortion, saying that natural law cannot take priority over the text of the constitution.[12]

But while natural law is certainly less frequently invoked now, judges may still have reference to 'higher law' principles in order to assist with constitutional interpretation. For example, in another case decided in 1995, the supreme court held that a gastronomy tube could be removed from a woman patient who had been in a near-persistent vegetative state for twenty-two years. In coming to this decision, the court referred to religious principles, noting the concept of the 'intrinsic sanctity of life' in deciding that 'a view that life must be preserved at all costs does not sanctify life'.[13]

Thus, although natural law theories no longer have the influence over judicial interpretation of the constitution as they once did, it would be inaccurate to suggest that contemporary constitutional interpretation comprises an exclusively secular approach. Rather, it appears that natural law doctrine may continue to have some bearing on future decisions.

The effect of the development of natural law doctrine by the judiciary has been to give judges a great deal more power than the framers of the constitution might have intended – leading in some cases to an undermining of the separation of powers doctrine, with judges essentially taking on a law-making role.

So it can be argued that there are two major obstacles in our path towards true republican status – lack of separation of powers and lack of separation of church and state.

How then can we move towards a more pluralist republican philosophy? Today's Ireland is a multi-cultural society, with an increasingly secular population growing ever more

disillusioned with revelations about abuses of power perpe-
trated by the institutional catholic church over the years.

Our laws should reflect this changing, more progressive
society. Unfortunately the latest constitutional referendum,
passed in 2004, represented a move backwards – towards a
narrower definition of 'citizenship' than previously existed,
towards a less generous vision of our republic, in which all
the children of the nation are not, it seems, to be cherished
equally after all.

In years to come, if we want to move forward, I believe
that we must be more inclusive in our approach. We must embrace the idea of Ireland as a community united behind the
need to ensure basic individual freedoms for all, regardless of
religion, class, gender, sexuality, race or nationality.

Our conception of the 'common good' should be premised
on the 'core norm' of equality, and our constitution should reflect that, rather than reflecting an outdated religious ethos.
We might look to the model of the new South African constitution, a dynamic text with a fundamental commitment to
ensuring equality. And we might look back to the core principles of republicanism, in order to reclaim and reinvigorate
the word 'republican' and the status of a 'republic' – in law
and in reality.

7

Republic: A Hope Mislaid?

Mary Kotsonouris

By the early years of the twentieth century there could have
been little doubt that an independent Ireland, in one form or
another, was on its way. It is clear from reading contemporary newspapers, correspondence and reports of public meet-
ings, that the Irish were about to rule themselves. The single-
mindedness and the expectation of the nationally-minded community are palpable, the sure and certain conviction that its
day had come. Roy Foster in *Modern Ireland* quotes the chief
secretary, Augustine Birrell, telling Asquith in 1915 that he
had discerned 'an increasing exaltation of spirit and a growth
of confidence'.[1] But there is little or no sense, then or later,
of a raging ambition to change civil society and to build a
new Jerusalem or perhaps the assumption was that it would
all follow automatically when the yoke of foreign rule was
broken. Even the Sinn Féin programme of 1905 – prim, worthy
and sober – smacks more of politburo than Che Guevara.[2]

One cannot say that, of course, about James Larkin and 1913 and the Dublin lock-out: there was certainly passion and rhetoric aplenty then in evidence. And noble aspirations beautifully expressed in the proclamation of 1916. Among the prisoners afterwards incarcerated in Ireland, Scotland and England and rigorously being directed by their camp leaders into a succession of self-help courses, were some men turning over ideas about the kind of society they wanted their people to live in?

Admittedly, there was the democratic programme of the first dáil, asserting heart-warming principles about the willing care of the aged and infirm and safeguarding of the physical and moral well-being of the nation whose children would not suffer want. Alas, it proved to be a false dawn, lasting no longer than the time taken to write down the words, the purpose being to allow the Labour party feel that it had made its contribution. As Brian Farrell has written elsewhere 'the promise spelled out therein remained a dead document as Ireland settled down to run its own affairs.'[3] The republic proclaimed in 1916 was to be a self-governing state, with or without a king and, apparently, not a community to be built from within.

After the treaty there was a great opportunity on the immediate horizon to reflect a new ethos, given to those who were about to establish the foundations of the state, that is, in the new legal regime to replace his majesty's judges of Saorstat Éireann. However, what was reflected was an extraordinary ambivalence, which had already been endemic in the subversive legal system which had flourished from 1919. The courts of Dáil Éireann, which had their beginnings in the local tribunals which sprang up to deal with land disputes in particular areas, were taken over by the ministry of home affairs, headed by Austin Stack, determined to mould them into a straitjacket of centralisation despite guerrilla warfare, martial law and the idiosyncrasies of judges and of litigants.[4] Of course it did not succeed: Stack's increasingly shrill missives were not so much ignored as worked around. The records of the parish courts remain an expression of the inventiveness of ordinary people in their efforts to bring order and fairness into their lives in the midst of chaos. It is not altogether fanciful to see an atavistic throwback to the Brehon Law ethos of restorative justice, a concept that has grown fashionable of late. The sentence on a man who stole a harness was to walk barefoot five miles across a mountain, carrying it on his shoulders. In a civil suit, the defendant was ordered to sow in his own garden the two rows of cabbage which his pig had eaten in the neighbour's.

The dusty files in the old public records office give the lie to Cicero's maxim that, in war, the laws are silent. The startling ambivalence of the subversive courts intended to undermine British rule in Ireland was that the laws administered therein were British. In the preamble to their constitution, Stack had written that, pending the enactment of a code of law by the dáil, citations could be made from early Irish law, the Code Napoleon, the Corpus Juris Civilis but not any from a text book published in Britain, a farcical piece of petty-mindedness, given not only their practice and procedures but the regular prosecutions taken under British statutes.[5] The novice politicians above in Dáil Éireann primarily saw the courts as an enormous propaganda coup, which, of course, they were, and moreover, returned yearly substantial revenue to the general dáil treasury. However, that did not stop the Provisional Government, in July 1922, closing them down overnight, when it interpreted the granting of a conditional order of *habeas corpus* as an affront to its authority.[6] (Who are we, then, to speak slightingly of banana republics?)

When the courts were abruptly abolished, a judiciary committee, as it was called, was appointed to draw up a plan for the free state courts to be established under the constitution. The person chosen by the executive to be the chairman was Lord Glenavy, a former lord chancellor and lord chief justice. Incidentally, as attorney general seven years previously, he had refused the prosecutor's plea that the 1916 leaders should be legally represented at their trial.[7] His appointment, which he himself does not appear to have considered particularly demanding, might have seemed a tactical decision to bring the legal establishment on side, although Glenavy could hardly have been a representative figure: one can only hope that it was not some aberrant sleveenism which made President Cosgrave conclude that no other lawyer was as qualified. To me, at any rate, the obvious person would have been Judge James Creed Meredith: he had been the guiding light of Dáil Éireann's legal regime, drafting the constitution for the dáil courts and the commission to wind them up and serving, in turn, as the head of both. And if it were of significance, just as grand a personage as Glenavy, although of a much finer intellect. Meredith, athlete, philosopher, gunrunner, lawyer, novelist, would be an extraordinary figure in any age or society, but his genius was taken for granted in his lifetime and has since been largely overlooked by legal historians.

In a letter to the committee in January 1923 Cosgrave denounced the legal administration (which was still in operation and of which the chairman had recently been head) as a 'standing monument of an alien government', English in its seed, in its growth and in its vitality: it had obliterated the 'native laws and institutions till then a part of the living natural organism', a graceful nod to Brehon law.[8] The people now had the greatly prized liberty 'to constitute a system of judiciary and an administration of law and justice according to the dictates of our own needs and after a pattern of our own designing'. If the latter phrase was intended to signal a radical re-drawing of the guidelines of the previous system, he was destined to be disappointed. Meredith, by far the most involved member of the committee, had urged that the laity should have some representation among all the lawyers, but only the president of the Dublin Chamber of Commerce was co-opted to stand in for the general public. The committee's report which appeared in May was brief and pragmatic, with but one real change proposed in the court hierarchy. The resulting bill was largely drafted by Arthur Creed

Meredith, a king's counsel. Behind the scenes there were already moves afoot, especially by senior figures in finance, to have the judges in the lower courts serve at the pleasure of government, which Hugh Kennedy, the attorney general, declared himself prepared to resist to the death. Nevertheless, the bill did make provision for the home affairs minister to exercise a control more suited to the civil service than to the judiciary.

Cosgrave, who was full of surprises, introduced the Courts of Justice Bill in the dáil on 31 July 1923. As there was an election due within days, he thought that it could be rushed through the dáil and seanad before dissolution and have the new courts up and running by Christmas. So he jettisoned the previous sentiments he had expressed about his majesty's judges and instead treated his listeners to the most extraordinary tribute to the administration of British justice in Ireland ever paid by an Irish nationalist. He prefaced it with a playful humility, that if he were only more competent in handling this sort of material:

> the concessions which I crave would be willingly assented to
> … The Bench in Ireland had the most distinguished and able
> jurists and conscientious lawgivers. So the Bill endeavoured to
> regulate the necessary alterations with as little disturbance and
> as free from offence as was possible under the circumstances.[9]

He assured the deputies that there were no great changes involved so that all concessions could be willingly assented to. After the long centuries of foreign rule, when independence had finally been won and with it the chance to build new institutions, the best that could be offered was more of the same with no offence given!

The president was not destined to get his own way: the passing of the Courts of Justice Bill in both the dáil and seanad was a struggle of titanic proportions. It has to be remembered that there would not be an official parliamentary opposition for several years. Had there been, it might have been a different debate. That would depend, to some extent, on how many lawyers Fianna Fáil brought into the dáil in 1927, because the discussion was primarily carried on by the lawyers in both houses. Tom Johnson, the Labour leader, was the only non-lawyer to put forward practical proposals, for instance, that the services of lay justices, which had been the outstanding feature of the dáil legal system, should be retained, and that a facility for pre-trial hearings would be useful in shortening litigation: his contribution was dismissed out of hand. (It may be worth mentioning, in passing, that the first small claims court, which has proved a great success, was set up in this jurisdiction less than a dozen years ago: truly the mills of God are as a thundering juggernaut compared to the pace of legal reform!)

The bill's principal innovation, borrowed from the courts of Dáil Éireann, was the new circuit court whose establishment was doggedly opposed by the barrister-legislators of both houses, since they thought (wrongly, as it turned out) that it would cut the umbilical cord with the law library, losing them prestige and income. They also strongly opposed any provisions which were discerned as government control over judges: these ranged from approval of the mode of dress for the higher judges to the payment of salaries to district justices by vote and not from the central fund. There was a solid consensus that in no way would the hated resident magistrates, serving at the whim of Dublin Castle, return in another guise. Cosgrave became increasingly annoyed at the unrelenting flow of amendments put forward and threatened to take the bill away from the oireachtas altogether and put it to a plebiscite. Nearly all the amendments were conceded in the end. One that was not – that justices of the district court should be called judges – eventually became law sixty-seven years later. Mr Cosgrave had counted on the bill being passed in a week: it had taken eight months – no wonder he was cross! The courts which we have today were established and the new judges sworn into office at Dublin Castle on 10 June 1924.

The *Freeman's Journal* hailed the end of 'the poison of social life' which was the previous justice system, where in every conflict between the civic rights of the common people and the interest of the dominant class, the scales were heavily weighed against the people. Presumably the leader writer thought those days were gone for ever. But was that the people's experience in their own courts? The variety and quantity of proceedings heard in our courts, over even a single decade, would make it impossible to form an opinion, and in any event, it has to be taken into account that losing parties understandably blame the court. However, a cursory glance at press reports of district court cases in different counties, from the 1920s to the 1960s, has made, at least, one reader profoundly relieved that there is now legal aid. One senses a kind of disdain for the poor or the inarticulate and a solidarity with the people of property. Admittedly, this is a superficial impression, but what is undoubtedly clear is the absence of interest in ongoing legal reform and, indeed, a lack of response to the few who did express an interest. Louis Walsh, a justice in Donegal who had served on the Judiciary committee, wrote of his disappointment in the way the circuit court, of which he had such hopes, had developed. Barristers had taken it over completely and solicitors were discouraged from appearing for clients, 'with a disdainful twitch of a gown', as he put it, so that the cheaper access intended to be provided to modest litigants had evaporated.

In 1940, James Creed Meredith, then a judge of the supreme court, read a paper to the Statistical and Social Enquiry Society urging a bewildering variety of reforms.[10] Regardless of the convention that sitting judges were not meant even to imply a criticism of the existing law, by way of a series of well reasoned arguments he dissected such questions as nationwide registration of title, a curb on testamentary freedom, a radical shake up in the law of evidence, the apportionment of civil liability: moreover, he considered the desirability of having examining magistrates to supervise the investigation of crime. Many of these changes did come about, albeit years later, but we still have to hear why the adversarial trial is preferable to the inquisitorial. He even had a page on the topical subject of whether vaccination should be compulsory.

During the discussion following his paper, he made an observation which is as relevant today as it was sixty years ago:

> I don't think there is much use asking the public to have respect for the law, if you, the Government, will not change a single bit of law that you know is bad unless there are votes in it.

Two years later, William Coyne, a justice in the west of Ireland who had served a prison sentence for his association with the dáil courts, expressed a similar opinion when he quoted the opinion of a legal writer:

> Furthermore, we can say that while ordinary people continue to regard the law and its intricacies as beyond them; while they remain in a mental state of impotence towards the law; and, so long as the subject remains outside the sphere of political interests, then the need for reform is not likely to be appreciated.[11]

In more recent times the people have seen the politicians interfacing directly with the administration of the law in the tribunals of enquiry which have become part of the political/legal landscape. While they may not be courts of law as such, since they were established by Dáil Éireann to hold specific enquiries, nevertheless they have the characteristics of a court and even the appearance of a trial. It will be a considerable time before we know the effect of these public hearings on the body politic and also on the politicians. Will it make them engage in a different way with the law's place in the well-being of society, or will lawyers begin to see themselves more clearly in the mirror which is being held up to their profession, and pause before launching the rhetoric of their defence?

One might have expected that enquiries into the conduct of its members would be carried out by a committee of the oireachtas: apparently, it is thought that party affiliation might cloud cool judgment (although such a forum worked for Parnell in another time and in another parliament). Hence we have had a succession of tribunals held, so appropriately, at Dublin Castle, with echoes for some, perhaps, of a Roman spectacle or of Salem or, for a very few, even, of the Committee of Public Safety. Not only can the people crowd in and watch it all happening; they can listen to nightly re-enactments on their radios. Is it too fanciful to suggest that they are witnessing the equivalent of their rulers, stripped of elegant shoes and socks, walking barefoot across the mountain? In 1949 we declared ourselves a republic. In a way, we might now be witnessing what true republicanism is about: the vindication of the equal worth of every citizen before the law and in society.

And when it is all over – and with apologies to Seamus Heaney – will we, judges and rulers alike, weep to atone for our presumption to hold office?[12]

8

From Republican Theory to Public Policy

Philip Pettit

The republican idea of freedom

Imagine that your welfare depends in some important way on the decision of others and you have no come-back against that decision. You are in a position where you will sink or swim, depending on their say-so. And you have no physical or legal recourse, no recourse even in a network of mutual friends, against them. You are in their hands, at their mercy. They can deal with you just as they will, depending on their arbitrary whims. In such a case you will suffer what the Romans called *dominatio* or domination; the persons on whose mercy you depend will be a *dominus* or master in your life.

The experience of such domination by another comes in many forms. Think of the child of the emotionally volatile parent; the wife of the occasionally violent husband; or the pupil of the teacher who forms arbitrary likes and dislikes.

Think of the employee whose security requires keeping the boss or manager sweet; the debtor whose fortunes depend on the caprice of money-lender or bank-manager; or the small business owner whose viability depends on the attitude taken by a bigger competitor or even a union boss. Or think, finally, of the welfare recipient whose fortunes turn on the mood of the counter-clerk; the immigrant whose standing is vulnerable to the whims that rule politics and talk-back radio; the older person who is vulnerable to the unrestrained gang of youths in her area; or the young offender whose fortunes depend on the whims of a judge or the choices of a vengeful lobby group.

In all of these cases a person is exposed to an arbitrary power of interference – a power of interfering at their own *arbitrium* or will – on the part of others. They suffer the presence of a master in their lives, even if not a master with a legal claim. I mention these instances of domination because if you concentrate your mind for a moment on what the experience of such domination is like, and if you let yourself imagine or remember the bitter taste of such subjection, such exposure, then you will put yourself in a good position to understand the core idea in republicanism. For the central theme in republican concerns throughout the ages – the theme that explains all their other commitments – has been a desire to arrange things so that citizens are not exposed to domination of this kind. They do not live, as the Romans used to say, *in potestate domini:* in the power of a master.

Roman republicans recognised that there were two sorts

of power or mastery that could induce domination, turn you into a slave or servant or subject, and induce the slavish, ingratiating mentality that they associated with such lack of standing. The one is the private power of other persons or groups, which the Romans called *dominium*. The other is the public power of the state itself, a power that they described as *imperium*. What they looked for was a dispensation of public power – a pattern of government – that would guard people against the private power of others, and so against domination by others, without itself becoming a dominating power in their lives: without itself having the aspect of a master. More of that institutional theme anon. For now let us return to the republican ideal of non-domination.

The main thing to say about this ideal is that it was expressed from the very first as an ideal of freedom. Roman republicans, and those who followed them later, identified freedom with the status people have when no one stands over them: when the civil and legal dispensation protects each against arbitrary interference by others – interference according to the will or *arbitrium* of others – and when it does so without itself having a power of arbitrarily interfering in their lives. They thought of freedom as the status you have, then, when you can walk tall among your fellows, look them squarely in the eye, and rejoice in knowing, and knowing that you are known, as someone who cannot be pushed around with impunity. You are incorporated, equally with others, in a common, effective field of mutual protection and empowerment. You are your own person, secure in the consciousness of commanding your own corner of the public space.

Republican freedom in this sense is more demanding than freedom in the contemporary, liberal sense of non-interference. You may manage to avoid interference – you may succeed in being let alone – while still living in the shadow of someone else's power; you may just be lucky enough or cunning enough to escape any interference from that quarter. Thus you may enjoy freedom in the contemporary diluted sense of non-interference, while still being unfree in the older sense of having to endure domination. For republicans the very existence of a power of arbitrary interference on the part of others is enough to make you unfree. For those of a later liberal stamp, power must be exercised against you before you lose your freedom. Republicans think of freedom as a status you command in relation to others – the standing that goes with not being subject to the arbitrary will of any other – whereas for liberals it tends to be seen as a matter of whether you actually manage to get your way.

The difference between the richer, republican understanding of freedom and this later, liberal construal of the ideal comes out nicely in the metaphor of free rein. For liberals freedom comes with not being reined in by any restraints on your activity. For republicans, however, free rein is the sort of thing that a rider gives a horse. It falls well short of freedom in the proper sense, because it implies that there is still a rider in place.

From the very beginnings of the tradition, republicans were outspoken in condemning the idea that you might achieve freedom just by courtesy of getting or winning such free rein. According to their way of thinking, to be in reins is already to be unfree, no matter how much slack is left in those fetters. It is to be in a position where you will inevitably have to keep a weather eye open for the moods of your masters; where you will have to practise self-censorship, even sycophancy, in order to keep them sweet; where, in short, you will have to live with the shoddy profile of deference and degradation that has been long associated with slavery, subjection, second-class citizenship. Freedom in the republican key is a rich and demanding ideal that is inconsistent with any such form of subjection.

The observation has practical implications. Under the classical liberal idea of freedom as non-interference – freedom as free rein – a woman might be as free as her husband, a servant as his master, even while enjoying little protection against their arbitrary power. Under the republican idea of freedom, as extended to women and servants, this could never be so. To be truly free the woman or the servant would have to command the respect of the husband or master, on pain of legal or cultural redress, not just happen to enjoy the benefit of his kindly disposition.

An old and Irish theme
I hope these remarks may help to make clear the sort of thing that is meant by republican freedom. I now want to say a little about the republican tradition in which this idea came to be nurtured and shaped.

From Republican Theory to Public Policy

Although many of the key ideas it deploys had Greek antecedents, republicanism was first kindled in classical Rome, when Polybius, Cicero and other commentators lauded the independence and non-domination that citizens could enjoy – citizens were restricted, of course, to mainstream propertied males – under Roman institutions. It was reignited in the renaissance of the 1400s and 1500s when the burghers of Italian cities like Venice and Florence prided themselves on how they could hold their heads on high in the Roman fashion and not have to beg anyone's favour. They were equal citizens of a common republic, so they felt, and were of a different political species from the cowed subjects of papal Rome or courtly France.

The republican flame passed to the English-speaking world in the seventeenth century when the 'commonwealth' tradition, which was forged in the experience of the English civil war, established and institutionalised the view that king and people each lived under the discipline of the same law. Monarchy did not have to be done away with, on this modernised version of republicanism, but it had to be made part of a constitutional order, and not allowed to become a centre of absolute power. Enthusiasts for the idea of a 'commonwealth' – an English word for 'republic' – argued that being protected by a fair law, no Briton was exposed to the arbitrary will of another, even the arbitrary will of the king; unlike the French and the Spanish, Britons were a race of sturdy and independent – even gruff and outspoken – freemen.

This argument rebounded, of course, on Britain's own fortunes. For in the eighteenth century their American colonists, equally gruff and outspoken, became persuaded that they themselves were denied their due freedom: they had to depend on the arbitrary will of a foreign parliament. Perhaps they had to pay only one penny in taxes to the London government, as a contemporary writer put it, but the government that took that one penny had the power to take also their last penny. Perhaps their British master was kindly and well-disposed, in other words used at the time, but the subjects of a kindly master were subjects still; they did not have the immunity to arbitrary power that true freedom requires. The American colonists sought to escape British domination by severing their ties with the home country and by establishing the world's first large, self-described republic.

The American precedent, and indeed the British model of a constitutional monarchy, helped to inspire the creation in the 1790s of the French republic. This second great revolution led, notoriously, to a reign of terror but it was born of the same desire to free ordinary people from subjugation to their would-be betters. Freedom as non-domination, as the French tradition spelled it out, required equality and indeed fraternity. It called for a scenario in which each could walk tall, secure in the knowledge that no one could lord it over them. Each could count on the support of others against any would-be dominating power. And so each could look others in the eye, seeing a fellow-citizen there, and not anyone possessed of special privileges. No one had to live at the mercy of another, no one had to hang on the grace and favour of a lord.

I said that you will be able to understand republicanism if you have a good sense of what domination means and of why it is abhorrent. Whether in classical Rome, renaissance Italy, seventeenth century England or eighteenth century America and France, all republicans saw such domination as the great evil to be avoided in organising a community and a polity. They thought of freedom as the supreme political value and they equated freedom with not being stood over by anyone, even a benevolent and protective master. To enjoy republican freedom was to be able to hold your head on high, to look others squarely in the eye, and to relate to your fellows without fear or deference.

But republicanism in the broad sense of a commitment to this vision of freedom was not just a British or American or French fashion, for it gained an early hold on our own Irish traditions. The volunteers who formed in the late 1770s – in part, ironically, to defend Ireland against the Americans – were an important conduit whereby the ideas we have been discussing gained roots here. The volunteers campaigned for repeal of the laws whereby the English parliament could overturn the laws of the Dublin parliament, and won this repeal in the 'constitutional settlement', as it was seen, of 1782. And then, just as the Americans were unsatisfied with exposure even to the possibility of heavier taxes being imposed by London, the volunteers announced themselves unsatisfied just with the repeal of such laws; they argued for, and they won, the renunciation of the claim ever to be able to rule over Ireland. Yet rule over Ireland – even Ireland of Grattan's par-

liament – England continued by various means to do. And
so, in response, those Volunteers, mainly of dissenting or pres-
byterian stock, joined forces with catholic and other groups
and in the early 1790s formed the first republican movement
in Ireland: that of the United Irishmen.

This movement was dominated by the figure of Theobald Wolfe Tone and his writings are shot through with the
sorts of republican ideas we have been discussing. He was an
afficionado and devotee of the core idea that no one who
was subject to the will of another – no individual and no community – could count as free, no matter how kindly the master.
'True republicans fight only to vindicate the rights of equality', he said, 'and detest ever the name of a Master'. 'I would
live in no country by the permission of a superior', he wrote
to a friend: 'I would live in no country just by the leave of the
authorities; I would only live there if I could live there as of
right.' He saw, as all republicans had seen, that to enjoy the
respect that goes with freedom, one has to command that respect. To enjoy respect only by grace and favour is to have to
depend on that grace and favour. It is to live under the shadow of another's power and so it is to be unfree.

From republican freedom to republican institutions
I have talked so far of two themes: the core republican idea
of freedom as non-domination, and the long history of that
idea in the annals and the achievements of Roman and neo-
Roman republicanism – Irish republicanism included. Let
me turn finally to a third theme, and one which explains

why I have called this essay 'From republican theory to political policy'. I want to emphasise that embracing the republican idea of freedom as non-domination means adopting a position with significant implications for how the state should be organised, and for how it should operate.

The Romans, as mentioned earlier in this talk, identified two distinct dangers for freedom as non-domination: the danger associated with private power or *dominium*, and the danger linked to public power or *imperium*. Following this lead, republicans will look for a state that can operate effectively against private domination, helping to reduce the degree of domination people suffer at the hands of other individuals and groups. And they look for a state that is organised in such a way that it will not itself represent a source of domination in people's lives. This will be a state that is conducted for the public interest, that pursues its policies in the public eye, and that acts under public control – a state that is truly a *res publica*, a matter of public business.

How is the republic of this ideal vision to operate? How is it to promote the freedom as non-domination of its citizens: that is, of the citizenry as a whole, not just a citizenry confined, as it was traditionally confined, to mainstream, propertied males? I mention just two aspects of what republicanism is bound to require on this front, setting aside a number of complex issues such as questions of international relations. Republicanism would require, first, a state that provides empowerment in face of the frailty and misfortune to which our species is susceptible; and second, a state that provides protection and vindication – protection and vindication of one's status as a citizen – against the ravages that criminal action may impose. First, a state that promotes social justice; and second, a state devoted to ensuring criminal justice.

Let me take criminal justice first. One of the main issues in contemporary politics is how to organise the protection of citizens against the domination of the criminal, whether that be the blue-collar or white-collar offender or the offender of a terrorist stamp. If we prize republican freedom as non-domination, then we can see quite clearly the different evils that crime represents and we can begin to see at least the broad direction that a criminal justice system ought to take.

Crime, to mention a first evil, almost always involves one or more people assuming the position of a dominator in relation to a victim or victims; it involves a denial of the person's status as someone incorporated in the republic. Second, crime imposes, or usually imposes, a material cost on victims and their families, whether that be a physical, financial or psychological loss. And third, crime challenges the community as a whole, suggesting that the republic in which people are meant to be empowered and protected is actually failing them.

This republican audit of the evils of crime gives us broad lines on which to think about criminal justice. It suggests that we should see the criminal justice system as a system for preventing and so far as possible rectifying the evils of crime. How much should we spend on prevention? That will depend on the extent to which preventive measures themselves threaten peoples freedom as non-domination or impose costs that undermine that freedom. What sorts of measures should it put in place for rectifying the evils of crime? Measures, broadly, that will serve so far as possible to restore the victim to his or her status as an undominated subject; to make compensation for their material loss; to restore the assurance of the community that the crime may have undermined; and to do all of this while recognising the claims of the defendant and the potential for that person's reinstatement in society.

The state that pursues such criminal justice comes across like a utopian ideal in the context of current regimes, mindlessly and counterproductively punitive as they routinely tend to be. But the state that pursues social justice, such as republicanism would also support, is one that we can at least dimly discern – alas, more and more dimly discern – in existing dispensations. This is the state that would provide directly or indirectly for the basic infrastructure needed to support people in the enjoyment of non-domination.

Suppose that someone is educationally disadvantaged or lacks access to proper sources of information about the opportunities available in their society. Suppose they live in chronic uncertainty about having the basic resources of shelter or sustenance. Or suppose that they do not have the assurance of medical support in the event of emergency or the wherewithal to make legal claims or mount a legal defence in response to the claims or charges that are brought against them. In any such instance, people's enjoyment of freedom as non-domination will be severely jeopardised. They will be easy pickings for the predators and they will have no chance of attaining the sort of status or standing that republicans associate with freedom.

These remarks on criminal and social justice should give some rough sense of how republicans will want the state to operate; of what ends it will want the state to pursue, as it seeks to reduce the domination that people are likely to suffer at the hands of others. But how will republicans want the state to be organised, so that it does not itself represent a source of domination in people's lives? The state will have to interfere with people, as in imposing taxation, setting up coercive law and punishing those who offend against that law. But can it be organised, as republicans have always wanted, so that in the pursuit of these activities it does not have the profile of an arbitrary power?

The challenge is a difficult one, given the recognition, deep in the tradition, that the state is a two-edged sword. Unless it is checked and limited to the pursuit of demonstrably common concerns, then it may itself prove a worse danger to people's freedom as non-domination than any danger it purports to guard against. If the state gives unfettered power to a single person, for example, as under an absolute monarchy or dictatorship, then that person will be able to interfere at will in people's lives and will dominate each and every one of them. Or if the state allows a particular faction or class to control what is done in its name, then the state will have that same dominating power in relation to those outside the class.

The problem here was phrased from early on in a famous question or quandary. *Quis custodiet ipsos custodes?* Who will police the police; who will watch the watchers; who will govern the governors? That problem was taken to be serious because republicans have been invariably conscious of the potential of power to corrupt those who wield it. As Lord Acton later expressed the idea: 'All power tends to corrupt; absolute power corrupts absolutely'. Wolfe Tone himself sounded the theme in a letter from America, reflecting on the danger of having too strong a president. 'Power long exercised', he said, 'would corrupt an Angel'.

The republican argument on this front has always been that the state must be so structured and constrained that it can act to further only what is by all lights in the common interest. It must not be free to serve the interests of a particular person or family or faction – even if that faction be a majority of the population – to the detriment of the interests of others. For if it is, then it will represent a dominating power in the lives of those others. Far from promoting their freedom overall – though it may do something in this way – its net effect will be to reduce that freedom: to make them into a subjected, systematically vulnerable class.

What constraints has republicanism generally favoured? The most prominent constraint in early Rome, and in the period of the American and French revolutions, was a constraint against monarchy but this ceases to be so prominent once we recognise the possibility of a constitutional monarchy. The more relevant considerations that the tradition has supported are ones that are just as important today as they were in classical Rome, renaissance Italy, or eighteenth century America or France. Let me mention some salient examples of such considerations:

1] the desirability of those in government being popularly elected, so that different parts of the populace have their rival interests represented;

2] the ideal of limiting the tenure of those in executive office, say by requiring their selection to be regularly renewed, as under periodic elections;

3] the need for government to rule by law, not in a case-by-case fashion, and to ensure that its laws apply to everyone, legislators included;

4] the indispensability of dividing up power, so that each authority is subject to checks and balances, and no one holds all the reins of power;

5] the requirement that whatever decisions are made by government are backed up by reasons deriving from purportedly common interests;

6] the capacity for ordinary citizens to question and contest the proposals and actions of government on the grounds that they are not adequately supported by such reasons; and

7] the reliance of this whole system on the existence of an active, concerned citizenry who invigilate the exercise of government power, challenge its abuses and if necessary seek office in order to put them right.

Most of these constraints are familiar in current democratic and constitutional theory, since that theory has been powerfully shaped by the republican tradition. But it is worth re-emphasising their importance, and seeking out ways whereby they may be improved. The contemporary focus on electoral democracy sometimes leads enthusiasts to suggest that the people can collectively do no wrong: that whatever the people electorally mandate is what the government ought to implement. But this is deeply anathema to republican ways of thought. Starting from the importance of freedom as non-domination, republicans must insist that just as that ideal requires a dispensation of social and criminal justice, so it requires a regime in which those ends are pursued in an open and contestable manner – in a manner, in particular, that allows even minorities to interrogate and contest any policies in which they discern the influence of purely selfish or factional interests.

The notion of *contestability* provides a good note on which to end this short set of reflections on what our traditional republicanism, properly understood, would require of us today. On the constitutional front, the great contemporary cry is for electoral democracy. Republicans must applaud that demand, seeing competitive elections – at least when they are not warped by the outrages of campaign financing – as a way of enabling ordinary people to have a say. But republicans will also insist that electoral democracy is worth little or nothing except in so far as it is complemented by a contestatory democracy: a democracy that is characterised by people's ability to call government to book, whether in the courts, in parliament, before inquiries or commissions, in the papers or on the streets.

The eighteenth century Scottish thinker, Adam Ferguson, expressed the republican line well when he said that what is needed for ensuring the freedom of individuals is not just a fine constitution but 'the recalcitrant zeal of a turbulent people'. Wolfe Tone had the same thought in mind when he looked for a world where 'constitutional liberty is studied and known, where the influence of the Crown is, comparatively, much weaker than with us, and where there is, out of doors, a jealous vigilance, a fund of knowledge, and a spirit of resistance not yet to be found in Ireland' (Cronin and Roche 1972, *Freedom the Wolfe Tone Way*, p. 87). 'The price of liberty is eternal vigilance', in the most hallowed of republican clichés. And vigilance, on a republican understanding, is what democracy must ultimately seek to encourage and employ.

To recap briefly, then, on what I have been saying. We have seen that the idea of freedom as non-domination is at the core of the republican theory; we have tracked the influence of that idea in republicanism as it appeared in the different forms associated with classical Rome, renaissance Italy, seventeenth century England, eighteenth century America, France and Ireland; and we have looked at some of its implications for how the state should operate and for how it should be organised.

Republicanism is a precious part of our heritage and I hope that what I, and others, have been saying may help to show that it is too important to be left to historians. It represents a complex of ideas that can guide Irish political thought, and political practice, in the future, as it has often guided it in the past.

The Contributors

Eunan O'Halpin Ph.D is Bank of Ireland Professor of Contemporary Irish History at Trinity College, Dublin, where he is also Director of the Centre for Contemporary Irish History. His research interests lie in recent Irish and British history and in intelligence studies

Marianne McDonald is Professor of Theatre and Classics in the Department of Theatre and Classics programme at the University of California San Diego, and a member of the Royal Irish Academy.

Iseult Honohan is a Lecturer in Political Theory in the Politics Department, University College Dublin.

Thomas Bartlett is Professor of Modern Irish History at University College Dublin.

Martin Mansergh is a senator, Seanad Éireann.

Brian Hanley graduated with a PhD from Trinity College Dublin and is now Lecturer in Irish History at NUI Maynooth.

The Contributors

Fintan O'Toole is a writer, and a columnist with *The Irish Times*.

Ivana Bacik is Reid Professor of Criminal Law at Trinity College Dublin and a practising barrister.

Mary Kotsonouris is a solicitor by profession. She served as a judge in the Dublin Metropolitan District.

Philip Pettit teaches political theory and philosophy at Princeton University, where he is William Nelson Cromwell Professor of Politics and Human Values.

Mary Jones is a producer working in the independent sector and is director of ArkHive Productions. Her academic background is in the social sciences, and she is author of *These Obstreperous Lassies: A History of the Irish Women Workers Union* (1988).

Notes

Ancient Republics

1 *Process and Reality: An Essay in Cosmology*, eds. D. R. Griggin and Donald W. Sherburne (1929; rpt. New York: The Free Press, 1985), pt. 2, ch. 1, p. 39.

2 There are many books about or translating Plato's *Republic*. I will cite four: Francis MacDonald Cornford, trans., int., and annotated, *The Republic of Plato* (1941; rpt. London/Oxford/New York: Oxford University Press, 1971–2); Allan Bloom, trans., int., annotated, *The Republic of Plato* (1968; rpt. New York: Basic Books/Harper Collins, 1991); G. R. F. Ferrari, ed. Tom Griffith, trans. *Plato/The Republic* (2000; rpt. Cambridge: Cambridge University Press, 2004); Nicholas P. White, *A Companion to Plato's Republic* (1979; rpt. Indianapolis/Cambridge: Hackett Publishing Company, 1980).

3 Apostolos N. Athanassakis, trans., int. and annotated, *Hesiod, Theogony/Works and Days/Shield* (1983; rpt. Baltimore/London: Johns Hopkins University Press, 1991), lls. 110–127, p. 70.

4 McDonald, Marianne summary from the text: *Aeschyli septem quae supersunt tragoedias*, Denys Page, ed. (Oxford: Clarendon Press, 1973), Pro. 447–506, pp. 306–8.

5 This is variously quoted. Gandhi evidently said this often during his lifetime, and varied the wording. It is quoted by Richard Attenborough in his film *Gandhi* (1982). See http://www.worldofquotes.com/

6 Quoted by E. F. Schumacher in *Good Work* (London: Jonathan Cape 1979).

7 McDonald, Marianne, translation of Sophocles' *Antigone* (London: Nick Hern Books, 2000), pp. 15–16.

8 McDonald, Marianne translation is based on the text edited by James Diggle, *Euripidis Fabulae*, in three volumes (Oxford: Oxford Classical Texts, 1984–1994); *Supplices/Iketides* in *Euri-*

Notes

pidis Fabulae, ed. J. Diggle II (Oxford: Clarendon Press, 1981).
9 *Aristophanes' Ecclesiazusae*, ed., trans. and comm. Alan H. Sommerstein (Warminster, Wiltshire: Aris & Phillips, 1998).
10 *Ibid.*, p. 12.

Reclaiming the Republican Tradition

1 For a more detailed overview of the theoretical tradition and its modern articulations, see Iseult Honohan, *Civic Republicanism*, London: Routledge (2002); and for alternative perspectives see Richard Dagger *Civic Virtues*, Oxford: Oxford University Press (1997), Philip Pettit, *Republicanism*, Oxford: Oxford University Press (1999) and Michael Sandel, *Democracy's Discontent*, Cambridge, MA: Harvard University Press (1996).
2 For Hobbes' critique of republicanism, see Thomas Hobbes, *Leviathan* (Harmondsworth: Pengiun, 1968 [1651]), especially Chapters 21 and 29.
3 James Harrington, *The Commonwealth of Oceana and A System of Politics*, Cambridge: Cambridge University Press (1992 [1656]), p. 8.
4 Nicolo Machiavelli, *The Discourses* (B. Crick, ed.), Harmondsworth: Penguin (1983 [1531]), p. 253.
5 Jean-Jacques Rousseau, *The Social Contract*, Harmondsworth: Penguin (1968 [1762]), p. 140.
6 James Madison, cited in Sandel, *op. cit.*, p. 132.
7 Rousseau, *op. cit.*, p.60
8 Mary Wollstonecraft, *A Vindication of the Rights of Women*, Harmondsworth: Penguin (1992 [1792]) and *Political Writings* (Oxford: Oxford University Press [1994]).
9 J. G. A. Pocock, *The Machiavellian Moment* (Princeton: Princeton University Press (1975)], p. 64.
10 *Guide Républicain* (Paris: Delagrave 2004).
11 This was powerfully criticised by Seán O'Faoláin as a betrayal of the wider republican tradition. See Mark McNally, 'Seán O'Faoláin's discourse of "the betrayal of the Republic" in mid-twentieth century Ireland' in *Republicanism in Theory and Practice* (I. Honohan and J. Jennings, eds) London: Routledge (2005).

12 Hannah Pitkin, 'Justice: on relating public and private, *Political Theory*, vol. 9, No. 3 (1981), p. 344.

13 J. K. Galbraith, *The Affluent Society*, Harmondsworth: Penguin (1958).

14 In interview with Carrie Crowley, RTE *Snapshots* (2002)

References

Dagger, R. (1997) *Civic Virtues*, Oxford: Oxford University Press

Galbraith, J. K. (1958) *The Affluent Society*, Harmondsworth: Penguin.

Guide Républicain (2004) Paris: Delagrave.

Harrington, J. (1992 [1656]) *The Commonwealth of Oceana and A System of Politics*, Cambridge: Cambridge University Press.

Hobbes, T. (1968 [1651]) *Leviathan*, Harmondsworth: Penguin.

Honohan, I. (2002) *Civic Republicanism*, London: Routledge.

Machiavelli, N. (1983 [1531]) *The Discourses* (B. Crick, ed.), Harmondsworth: Penguin.

McNally, M. (2005) 'Seán O'Faoláin's discourse of 'the betrayal of the Republic' in mid-twentieth century Ireland' in *Republicanism in Theory and Practice* (I. Honohan and J. Jennings, eds) London: Routledge.

Pettit, P. (1999 [1997]) *Republicanism*, Oxford: Oxford University Press.

Pitkin, H. (1981)'Justice: on relating public and private, *Political Theory*, vol. 9, No. 3, pp. 327–52.

Pocock, J. G. A. (1975) *The Machiavellian Moment*, Princeton: Princeton University Press.

Rousseau, J. J. (1968 [1762]) *The Social Contract*, Harmondsworth: Penguin.

Sandel, M. (1996) *Democracy's Discontent*, Cambridge, MA: Harvard University Press.

Wollstonecraft, M. (1992[1792]) *A Vindication of the Rights of Women*, Harmondsworth: Penguin.

_____(1994) *Political Writings*, Oxford: Oxford University Press.

Notes

Theobald Wolfe Tone and Irish Republicanism and Separatism

1 This discussion of Tone's thought, unless otherwise stated is drawn from my 'The Burden of the Present: Theobald Wolfe Tone, Republican and Separatist' in David Dickson, Daire Keogh, Kevin Whelan (ed), *The United Irishmen* (Dublin, 1993), pp. 1–15: full scholarly support for the arguments advanced will be found in the notes to this article.

2 Frank MacDermot, *Tone and his Times* (London, 1939), p. 269; Tom Dunne, *Theobald Wolfe Tone: Colonial Outsider* (Cork, 1982), pp. 16-17, 23, 47.

3 Marianne Elliott, *Wolfe Tone: Prophet of Irish Independence* (New Haven, 1989), pp. 4, 37.

4 W. T. W. Tone (ed), *Life of Theobald Wolfe Tone* (2 vols., Washington 1826), ii, p. 64.

5 Elliott, *Tone*, p. 419.

6 Hubert Butler, *Wolfe Tone and the Common Name of Irishman* (Dublin, 1985), p. 9.

7 Tone, *Life*, i, p. 499 (my emphasis).

James Connolly and the Worker's Republic

1 James Connolly, *Labour In Irish History* (London, 1987), p. 25.

2 Fintan Lane, *The origins of modern Irish socialism* (Cork, 1997).

3 Connolly, *Labour*, p.166.

4 Emmet O'Connor, *A labour history of Ireland*, (Dublin, 1992) p. 101–8.

5 Henry Patterson, 'Fianna Fáil and the working-class: the origins of the enigmatic relationship' in *Saothar* 13 (1988), pp. 81– 88.

6 James Connolly, *Collected Works* (Dublin, 1987–88), Vol. 1, p. 36.

7 James Hyland, *James Connolly* (Dundalk, 1997) provides a lively introduction to Connolly's life and work. For a good selection of Connolly's journalism see Aindrias Ó Cathasaigh, *The Lost Writings, James Connolly* (London, 1997).

8 *History Ireland*, Vol. 3, No. 2, Summer 1995, pp. 44–47.

9 *Collected Works*, Vol. 1, p. 466–9.

10 *Ibid.*, Vol. 2, p. 212.

11 W. K. Anderson, *James Connolly and the Irish Left* (Dublin, 1994), p. 69.

12 *Collected Works*, Vol. 1, p. 337.

13 Anderson, pp. 58–66.

14 *Ibid.*, pp. 16–24.

15 Hyland, p.31.

16 R. D. Edwards., *James Connolly* (Dublin, 1981), p. 35–36.

17 *Collected Works*, Vol. 2, p. 211.

18 *Ibid.*, Vol. 1, p. 311.

19 Austen Morgan, *James Connolly – a Political Biography* (Manchester, 1988), p. 196–203.

20 *Collected Works*, Vol. 1, p. 467.

21 Connolly, *Labour*, p. 20–22.

22 *Collected Works*, Vol. 1, p. 307.

23 Hyland, p. 47.

24 Pádraig Yeates, *Lockout-Dublin 1913* (Dublin, 2000), p. 220–221.

25 Morgan, p. 86–87.

26 In fact O'Connell's attitude to trade unionism was more complex than Connolly argued. Fergus O'Ferrell, *Daniel O'Connell* (Dublin, 1981), pp. 98–100, 108–110.

27 Hyland, p. 40–42.

28 Connolly, *Labour*, p. 167.

29 Brian Farrell, 'The First Dáil and its Constitutional Documents' in B. Farrell (ed), *The Creation of the Dáil* (Dublin, 1994), pp. 61–74.

30 Emmet O'Connor, *Syndicalism in Ireland, 1917–1923* (Cork, 1988).

31 Richard English, *Radicals and the Republic-Socialist Republicanism in the Irish Free State, 1925–37* (Oxford, 1994), p. 52–55.

32 Helen Litton, *The Irish Civil War* (Dublin, 1995), p. 28.

33 Brian Hanley, *The IRA, 1926–1936* (Dublin, 2002), pp. 14, 177.

34 B. Hanley, 'The Irish Citizen Army after 1916' in *Saothar* 28 (2003), pp. 37–47.

35 Emmet O'Connor, *Reds and the Green, Ireland, Russia and the Communist Internationals, 1919–43* (Dublin, 2004).

36 Mellows arguments against the treaty were more conventionally republican in the 1921–22 period. Michael Hopkinson, *Green Against Green-the Irish Civil War* (Dublin, 1988), pp. 37, 41, 59, 72, 101–2.

37 Fearghal McGarry, 'Catholics first and politicians afterwards':

'the Labour Party and the Workers Republic, 1936–39' In *Saothar* 25 (2000), p. 57–66.

38 Henry Patterson, *The Politics of Illusion – a Political History of the IRA* (London, 1997), p. 96–139.

The Unreal Republic

1 Arthur Mitchell and Pádraig Ó Snodaigh (eds.), *Irish Political Documents 1916–1949*, Irish Academic Press, 1985, p. 247.

2 Philip Pettit, *Republicanism: A Theory of Freedom and Government* (OUP 1997). See also the final essay of this series.

3 Both quotes are from Louise Fuller, *Irish Catholicism Since 1950*, Gill and Macmillan, Dublin, 2002, pp. 8–9.

Law in a Republic

1 *Dáil Éireann Debates*, Vol. 97; 17 July, 1945, columns 2569–70. For comment see Chubb, B., *Source Book of Irish Government*, Dublin: IPA, 1983, pp. 16–17.

2 *Seanad Éireann Debates* Vol. 36; 9 December, 1948, column 3.

3 *Ellis v. O'Dea (No. 1)* [1989] IR 530.

4 *Report of the Constitution Review Group*, Dublin: Government Publications, 1996.

5 [1972] IR 241.

6 *Crotty v. An Taoiseach* [1987] IR 713.

7 See Kelly, F., *A Guide to Early Irish Law*, Dublin: Dublin Institute for Advanced Studies, 1988.

8 Lalor, B. (ed), *The Encyclopaedia of Ireland*, Dublin: Gill and Macmillan, 2003, p. 172.

9 [1965] IR 294 (the case was heard in 1963).

10 See *Murtagh Properties v. Cleary* [1972] IR 330 (the right to earn a livelihood); *McGee v. Attorney General* [1974] IR 284 (the right to marital privacy). For discussion see Hogan, G. and Whyte, G., *The Irish Constitution*, Dublin: Butterworths, 2003 (fourth ed).

11 *Norris v. Attorney General* [1984] IR 36. The plaintiff subsequently won his case against Ireland at the European Court of Human Rights.

12 *Re Article 26 and the Regulation of Information (Services outside the State for the Termination of Pregnancies) Bill 1995* [1995] 1 IR 1.
13 *Re A Ward of Court* [1996] 2 IR 73.

Republic: A Hope Mislaid?

1 R. F. Foster, *Modern Ireland, 1600–1972*, London 1988, p. 476.
2 *United Irishman*, 9 December 1905.
3 Brian Farrell in the foreword to *Retreat from Revolution: The Dáil Courts, 1920–24*, Mary Kotsonouris, Dublin 1994.
4 Kotsonouris, *Retreat from Revolution*, Chapter 1.
5 NAI, DEEC 11/179, Rules and Forms of Parish and District Courts, Department of Home Affairs, 1921 (referred to as *The Judiciary*).
6 Colm Campbell, *Emergency Law in Ireland, 1918–1925*, Oxford 1994, p. 157.
7 Leon O'Broin, *W. E. Wylie and the Irish Revolution 1916–1922*, Dublin 1989, pp. 23–24.
8 UCD Archives, P4/1090.
9 *Dáil Debates*, vol. 4, c. 1716, 31 July 1923.
10 'Desirable Ameliorations of the Law' by Mr Justice James C. Meredith, D.Litt., *Journal of the Statistical and Social inquiry Society of Ireland, 93rd Session Vol XV] (1939–40)*, pp. 63–74. I am indebted to Professor Tadgh Foley of the University of Galway for his kindness in calling my attention to this article and in giving me a copy.
11 Liam Ua Cadhain, *The Law Courts in Éire*, Dublin, n.d., p. 69.
12 Seamus Heaney, *From the Republic of Conscience: New Selected Poems 1966–1987*, London: Faber 1990 p. 218.

Other Interesting Books

THE COURSE OF IRISH HISTORY

Edited by T. W. Moody and F. X. Martin

A revised and enlarged version of this classic book provides a rapid short survey, with geographical introduction, of the whole course of Ireland's history. Based on a series of television programmes, it is designed to be both popular and authoritative, concise but comprehensive, selective but balanced and fair-minded, critical but constructive and sympathetic. A distinctive feature is its wealth of illustrations.

THE GREAT IRISH FAMINE

Edited by Cathal Póirtéir

This is the most wide-ranging series of essays ever published on the Great Irish Famine and will prove of lasting interest to the general reader. Leading historians, economists, geographers – from Ireland, Britain and the United States – have assembled the most up-to-date research from a wide spectrum of disciplines, including medicine, folklore and literature, to give the fullest account yet of the background and consequences of the Famine.

MILESTONES IN IRISH HISTORY

Edited by Liam de Paor

Succinct and readable, *Milestones in Irish History* goes beyond the 'what' and 'when' to elucidate the 'why' of the troubled but fascinating course of Irish history.

Milestones in Irish History spans the whole range of Irish history from the megalithic era to the late twentieth century. Contributors include the leading experts in their fields, among them Frank Mitchell, J. J. Lee, John A. Murphy, Margaret MacCurtain and Ronan Fanning, who discuss such topics as:

- the building of Newgrange, Knowth and Dowth at the same time as the pyramids, 2500 BC

- the ending of the Gaelic order with the Flight of the Earls in 1607

- the death of the Irish language – an abandonment unique in world history

- the partition of Ireland in 1920, viewed as a short-term British solution to the 'Irish problem'.

Milestones in Irish History is an essential guide to the understanding of key epochs and events in Irish history.